BALLET

IS NOT FOR

MUSLIM

GIRLS

Growing up Pakistani-Canadian

by MARIAM S. PAL

Renaissance.
Diverse Canadian Voices

BALLET
IS NOT FOR
MUSLIM
GIRLS

Renaissance.
Diverse.Canadian Voices

Cover is photo of Mariam S. Pal taken by her father, Izzud-Din Pal. Cover and interior design by Nathan Fréchette. Edited by Lorenzo Carrara, Jenna Low and Nabiha Rasool.

Legal deposit, Library and Archives Canada, 2022.

Paperback ISBN: 978-1-990086-20-5
E-book ISBN: 978-1-990086-28-1
Audio ISBN : 978-1-990086-29-8

Renaissance Press - pressesrenaissancepress.ca

Printed in Gatineau

We gratefully acknowledge the precious support of the Canada Council for the Arts.

Conseil des Arts du Canada

Canada Council for the Arts

This book is dedicated to the millions
who rebuilt their lives after Partition.
It is also in memory of my parents,
Izzud-Din Pal and Catherine Telik Pal,
whose courage has always inspired me.

Preface

Ballet is not for Muslim Girls is a memoir of my childhood in Victoria, British Columbia, in the 1960s and 1970s. I was born in Montréal's Royal Victoria Hospital. My mother was a Polish-Canadian lapsed Catholic from Northern Ontario and my father was a secular Pakistani Muslim. Papa immigrated to Canada from Pakistan in 1955. His plan was to get a PhD in economics from McGill University and return to Pakistan. Instead, he married my Canadian mother, started a family, and lived in Canada until his death at the age of 88 in 2013.

My parents moved to Victoria, BC, in 1961 when my father accepted a teaching position at what was then Victoria College, now the University of Victoria. I grew up in Victoria and attended school and university there. In 1980, I left for Montréal and further studies at McGill.

In today's Canada, mixed marriages and multicultural families are common. In 1960s and '70s Canada, they were rare. In Victoria, BC, they were virtually nonexistent. There were no other children in my school whose fathers and mothers came from such different cultures or who looked like my parents did. Despite the fact that I was born in Canada, I struggled to establish my Canadian identity.

Very few Pakistanis settled in Canada in the 1950s. This was directly attributable to a racist Government of Canada quota on immigrants from India and Pakistan. Between 1951 and 1961, only a hundred visas were issued yearly to citizens of these two countries. After completing their studies, most Indians and Pakistanis returned to their home countries. Marriage to Canadians was unusual.

The brutal 1947 Partition of India was a constant presence in my father's life and by consequence, in the life of his family. It took sixty years for him to share with me what horrors my family had endured. The prologue explains my family history and how they survived Partition. This historical background is the backdrop to my father's life and to mine as well.

Most names have been changed although I use my grandfather's real name in several chapters.

My sister, Salma, at her own request, appears infrequently in this memoir.

I have prepared a glossary of the many Urdu words used throughout the book. While I have done my best to use these words in a context where their meaning will be fairly obvious, or not really matter, readers may find this useful.

TABLE OF CONTENTS

Prologue:
Partition's Child

My late father, Izzud-Din Pal in Lahore, likely from the late 1940s.

It all starts with Partition. I am Partition's child.

The soft knocking on the carved wood door of the *haveli* was persistent. "Pal *sahib*, Pal *sahib*! Please open the door!" Siraj-ud-Din Pal, my grandfather, held aloft a single candle as he walked towards the entry of the family home in Amritsar, India. It sputtered in the humid heat of an August evening. Slowly, cautiously, he slid open the door. He recognized the face through the flickering candlelight. It was his brother's friend, the tall Sikh. Swiftly, the Sikh stepped inside, silently closing the heavy door behind him.

"Pal *sahib*," he whispered, "it is very dangerous now. Please listen to me – your family must leave Amritsar immediately. Attacks on Muslim neighbourhoods are planned for tomorrow."

Siraj-ud-Din Pal looked down at the ground. He sighed. "So the time has come. Thank you, brother, for warning us."

"I will make sure you get out of here safely," the Sikh said. "You must be ready tomorrow morning at dawn. Stay in the house until I get here."

"We will be ready. I don't know how I can ever possibly repay you."

"Good night, Pal *sahib*." The Sikh opened the door and slid back into the clammy darkness of Wrestler Street.

A knock on the door changed my father's life forever. A few hours later, he and his family left Amritsar for Lahore in what would soon be the country of Pakistan. Partition made them refugees.

مریم

Partition was the division on August 14 and 15, 1947, of the colony of British India into India and a bifurcated Pakistan, West and East; Pakistan was to be a home for India's Muslims.

At first, the British planned a two-year transition, from 1946 to 1948. But on June 2, 1947, bleeding and broke from World War II, they decided to squeeze two years to ten weeks. The new date was August 15, 1947. Lord Mountbatten,

Viceroy of India, chose the anniversary of the defeat of the Japanese in World War II to partition India. If he was aware that the Partition of India would coincide with the August monsoon and the Muslim holy month of *Ramadan*, he didn't say so.

Eid, the biggest Muslim holiday of the year, marking the end of *Ramadan* fasting, was on August 17, 1947. Pakistan was three days old. The timing was equivalent to Scotland leaving the UK between Christmas and New Year's.

A British barrister, who had never been further east than Paris, was appointed to draw the border between India and Pakistan. The Viceroy would only announce the official map two days after independence.

Partition should have been good news to the Indians who had struggled for decades for self-rule. Instead, my family and millions of others feared they would be stuck on the wrong side of the border. The Muslim Pals lived in Amritsar, a Sikh holy city that was sure to become part of India on Independence Day. Nearly half of Amritsar's population was Muslim; in the mid-1800s, Kashmiri weavers and carpet traders were attracted by the city's status as a major trading centre and stayed, helping it flourish.

In an escalating panic, fifteen million people migrated between India and Pakistan. Muslims mostly went west, to Pakistan, and Hindus and Sikhs east, to India. Communities that had lived peacefully for generations turned on each other in a savage orgy of ethnic cleansing; more than seventy years later historians struggle to explain why. A million lives were lost, and thousands were injured, missing, or maimed. Thanks to their friend's warning, my family fled for Lahore, in what would soon be Pakistan, just five days before independence.

Lahore is only twenty miles west of Amritsar; in 1947, the rail journey through flat farmland and forest lasted thirty-five minutes. My father's friends reminisced about going by rail from Amritsar to Lahore to go to the movies or for a shopping trip in the city many referred to as "the Paris of India." Trains operated between the two cities from early morning until late at night, fares were cheap, and the ride was safe.

In the anarchy of the summer of 1947, these trains turned into death traps on wheels that took hours, sometimes days, to reach their destination. Marauding gangs of Hindus, Sikhs, or Muslims brazenly ambushed what were mostly unguarded trains going in either direction. The thousands of British soldiers that had traditionally kept order in colonial India for hundreds of years had all gone home as Britain had not anticipated any large-scale movements of people. New armies and police were established only after the two countries became independent. In the security vacuum that ensued, the summer of 1947 turned brutal as rail carriages pulled into Lahore or Amritsar stations dripping with blood and loaded with a daily cargo of decomposing and mutilated bodies. Often, "A Present from India" or, "A Present from Pakistan" was scrawled in chalk on the side of the engine.

مریم

When I was a child, my father would sometimes talk about Partition. He would share a vignette, like the tale of the Sikh friend knocking on the door. Then he would stop and refuse to say anything more. For many years, I asked my father to tell me the whole story. I wanted to know what happened in 1947. But my father, whom I called Papa, adamantly refused to talk about it.

Then, in 2007, sixty years after Partition, he finally relented. On a hot July day, air conditioning purring in the background, we sat down over tea at the kitchen table in his condo.

Papa thumbed through a sheaf of papers in a dog-eared manila file folder. He wrote in pencil on scrap paper. Ever the organized academic, he made notes as he tried to remember the sequence of events that resulted in our family fleeing Amritsar in August 1947. He exhaled and looked down at his papers. Papa was twenty-two when Partition turned his whole life upside down. On that day in 2007, he was eighty-two. He shook his head and looked at me.

"Well, my dear, it's been sixty years. I tried to forget about it but since you want to know what happened, I will tell you."

"As the head of the household, *Abajee*, your grandfather, decided that the Pals would stay in Amritsar. The family had lived there for more than four generations. It was our home."

Papa explained that in the scorching hot summer of 1947, the pre-Partition riots grew increasingly violent. Like many affluent Amritsar families, the Pals planned to flee tempo-rarily to the nearby city of Lahore in what would soon be

Pakistan. *Dada Abajee* coordinated the preparations. My father already attended university in Lahore. Before returning to Amritsar for the summer, Papa rented a house in Lahore for the family from a Muslim landlord and furnished it with the bare necessities: *charpais* (the wooden framed rope bed typical of South Asia), a stove, and oil lamps. Middle Uncle brought some basic household supplies from Amritsar, including some cooking utensils, a couple of chairs for my grandparents, salt, spices, and bags of rice and lentils. They hid money and some of my grandmother's gold jewellery deep inside the rice and lentils. The Pals had a refuge, should one be needed.

مریم

Early on the morning of August 9, the Sikh arrived, driving a hearse. My family lived in a traditional Muslim house typical of northern India, called a *haveli*. The house had a private back entrance for the coach and buggy that the family had used before they acquired an automobile. This wide entrance easily accommodated the hearse.

My grandmother, one of my father's aunts, and five female cousins went to the railway station in this vehicle. The privacy of the hearse ensured their safety; many women were abducted on the streets during the Partition violence. Most never saw their families again.

My father, his two brothers, and his elder uncle went to the railway station separately, riding in a *tonga*, a two-wheeled horse-drawn cart common in the Punjab. My grandfather and younger great-uncle stayed behind to close their law office. They planned to join the family in a couple of days.

"Amritsar was tense," said Papa. "The trip to the station took half an hour but every second of it was nerve-wracking. There were roving gangs and we were afraid of encountering an angry anti-Muslim mob." Papa drew an imaginary sword across his throat. "That would have been the end of us."

But my family was lucky. Nobody stopped their *tonga* and soon the family was safely reunited at Amritsar railway station.

Papa remembered that, unusually, there was a heavy police presence at the railway station. "Perhaps they knew something."

My family of eleven boarded the train to Lahore with the clothes they were wearing and little else. The women hid some jewellery in their *shalwars*. How could they know that their clothes, cooking pots, furniture, and the accumulated flotsam and jetsam of family life had all been lost forever in the house they left behind?

Papa remembered *Dada Abajee*'s library – his priceless collection of Arabic and Persian manuscripts: "My father collected those manuscripts over his entire lifetime and many of them were very valuable. But there was no way we could take them with us. I had catalogued his entire collection for him and so I knew and appreciated just how precious it was.

"He never spoke of his library again. It was too painful."

The train to Lahore was packed with Muslims, but to his surprise, my father did not see anyone he knew. Amritsar's

Muslim community was small, and it was not unusual to bump into friends or distant relatives.

"I wondered if we were the last train of Muslims to leave Amritsar."

Papa, his two brothers, his mother, his uncle, aunt, and five female cousins sat on wooden benches inside the third-class train car. It was unbearably hot, and all of the windows were open. They had brought water with them but no food. The whistle blew as the steam train lumbered out of Amritsar station. The clammy monsoon air brushed against their faces, but it was not refreshing.

"What was it like on the train?" I asked.

"Nobody talked. We wondered if we would meet the same fate as some of the other trains. Would our train be attacked? My mother wept silently throughout the entire trip."

The train made several scheduled stops but was not attacked or ambushed.

Three excruciating hours later they arrived at the Lahore railway station and learned that theirs had been the last safe train to run from Amritsar to Lahore. They went to the rented house where they waited for my grandfather and his brother. Lahore swirled with rumors about what was happening in Amritsar.

My father went to the Lahore railway station several times a day looking for his father and uncle, in case they arrived by rail. But all he saw were silent steam trains parked in the station, bulging with bloody corpses rotting in the August heat. Infants and children, slaughtered, their mutilated bodies left to decay under the scorching sun.

The day after he arrived in Lahore, my father went to one of the city's Hindu neighbourhoods to warn his favourite professor, Brij Narayan, of the danger and to tell him to leave. He was too late: the house had been ransacked and Brij Narayan had disappeared, never to be heard from again.

I asked my father if he remembered the name of the Sikh friend who had alerted the family, but he shook his head. "It was just so long ago."

"Did you feel secure in Lahore once you got there?" I asked.

Papa did not mince words: "Yes, we were safe, but the Muslim vigilantes moved from Amritsar to Lahore. They did brisk business demanding protection money from Hindus and Sikhs who had stayed behind in Lahore. It was disgusting."

I wondered how the different religious communities had gotten along prior to Partition. Papa's answer surprised me.

"We were separate groups but equal. There was no daily tension between us until the spectre of Partition arose on the horizon. There was more tension between Sunni and Shia Muslims than there was between Muslims, Hindus, and Sikhs in the rest of the population. My lawyer father had clients from all groups.

مریم

Two days after my family left Amritsar, the Sikh friend drove my grandfather and his brother to a town called

Waga on what would soon be the India-Pakistan border. They found transport to Lahore and arrived safely at the rented house.

"Just a minute," said Papa. He rose from his chair and slowly walked to the living room. I followed him and watched as he took a small black frame off the wall. I recognized it. The title said, "Amritsar in 1947: Walled City." Papa had found a map of pre-Partition Amritsar in the Geography Department's map room, made a copy, and framed it. Standing beside him, I watched as he traced the Muslim neighbourhood where he had grown up.

"The streets were narrow and winding – if you took a turn you could end up in the Sikh or Hindu quarter. We all lived together, cheek by jowl, as the Brits would say. My father attended his Hindu clients' weddings and received gifts of food from Sikh clients during their festivals."

Papa pointed at the map. "Our house was on Wrestler Street, across from a mosque. The mosque was the centre of community life because it had a well and shower stalls for men in a city where many people lacked indoor plumbing. I attended primary and elementary school at this mosque's *madrassa*, later transferring to a public school. It was a wonderful education. I was encouraged to excel and to pursue further studies particularly in Urdu, Arabic, and algebra.

"There was our house, in a neighbourhood called *Kaira Karam Singh*. The nearest gate was the *Bhagtan-Wala* Gate."

Papa poured himself some more tea and took a sip.

"Life was prosperous and peaceful. But then things changed after the British announced they would be gone by the middle of August. Gangs of Muslim vigilantes – *goondas* – took control of the streets in the Muslim neighborhoods, demanding protection money."

"What did you do?"

Papa shrugged and looked up from his notes. "We were forced to pay our fellow Muslim brothers in order to stay safe. This was the beginning of my disillusionment with Partition – seeing the corruption start. It was Muslims exploiting Muslims. And another thing, all three groups – Hindus, Sikhs, and Muslims – were guilty of terrorizing and killing." He looked me right in the eye and waved his index finger. "Nobody's hands were clean."

مریم

One of my father's uncles returned to Amritsar a month after they had fled to Lahore. The family house had been burnt to the ground and a Hindu family was squatting in the ashes. Ironically, Muslim gangs, angry that my Muslim family had left without paying protection money, had torched the house.

Many friends from Amritsar were dead and their female relatives abducted and missing. The family could not return – they would have to start again in Lahore. My grandfather, great-uncle, and Big Uncle had lost their joint law practice that had been based in Amritsar. Daily, they would go to the Lahore courts trying to find new clients.

They also needed a house. Papa explained that the governments of India and Pakistan coordinated to compensate refugees for lost property. Refugees submitted sworn affidavits attesting to the size and value of the property they had lost in India. Once approved, this entitled them to receive abandoned property in Pakistan.

"The compensation for lost property became a farce," said Papa. "Many people saw it as a chance to enrich themselves, so they lied through their teeth about the supposed palaces they had lived in prior to Partition. The greed made me sick. This was the beginning of systemic corruption in Pakistan."

One of my father's uncles knew a lawyer who had gained possession of five houses, abandoned by Hindu lawyers, near the Lahore High Court. The friend suggested that our family move into one of the houses and squat there until they could get the paperwork completed. Vandals had stripped the house bare, except for law books strewn all over the floor. Two families moved into the large bungalow – my *Dada Abajee*, *Ami Jee*, my grandmother, and their three sons, as well as my father's younger uncle, a criminal lawyer, and his family.

After my father's death I found a grainy photocopy of a document in his personal papers entitled "Record of Permanent Transfer." This document, signed by the Settlement Commissioner, recorded the steps that the family went through to legally acquire the property. The process only began twelve years after Partition, in 1959, and was finally completed on December 2, 1965. The Pals were squatters for eighteen years.

In the weeks after Papa told me the family story, I became obsessed with Partition. I watched old newsreels and film footage from 1947 on YouTube over and over. As I looked at cloudy film of a train leaving Amritsar station in August 1947,

I wondered if it was the train my family was on. Was that our family home in the faded photograph of a charred house in Amritsar?

Six years after I heard my father's story, an essay I wrote about my family's survival of Partition was published in a Canadian newspaper: sixty-six years to the day that my family fled Amritsar. By coincidence, it was also *Eid*, celebrating the end of a month of fasting during *Ramadan*.

I did not tell my father that my article was going to be published but when I phoned him that morning, he had read it and was pleased. A week or two later I asked him some more questions about Partition. He reluctantly answered them. The next time he told me that he was getting old and that he didn't want to talk about Partition anymore. I stopped asking.

A couple of months after my article appeared, a good friend of my father's, Lee, rang me.

"I saw your article in the paper. I was happy that it was published. If it hadn't been for your father, I would never have known about Partition. I've been meaning to call you."

Lee continued, "One part of your article was very different from what your father told me about Partition."

Curious, I asked, "What part was that?"

"Your father told me that the train between Amritsar and Lahore was attacked by Hindu or Sikh gangs. He hid under some dead bodies in the train. Incredibly, he survived."

I decided to talk to my father about it when I felt the timing was right. But that moment never came. Three weeks after my conversation with Lee, my father died. I will never know for sure, but I like to think that my father was sparing his children the grisly details of how horrific Partition was. The more I read, the more I realized that my father deliberately left out the most brutal and traumatic memories. Perhaps Papa pushed them into some dark, deep corner of his mind.

I am not willing to accept that I will never know what really happened to my father more than seventy years ago. Two editorials about my family's Partition story published in Indian newspapers have yielded many touching stories, but I have yet to identify the mystery Sikh man who helped the Pals.

In 2016, with the help of an Indian researcher, I was able to identify the family home in Amritsar. I planned a visit for November 2016. I wanted to visit the site of the family home and hoped to find the graves of my ancestors and visit other locations important to the history of the Pal family.

My plan to visit was foiled. The Government of India would not issue me, a Canadian, with a visa. They considered me to be Pakistani and not Canadian because my father and grandparents migrated to Pakistan in 1947. Although I do not hold a Pakistani passport nor have I ever lived in Pakistan, I was told I had to request the Government of Pakistan to issue me a security clearance. Only then would the Government of India, in a bizarre bureaucratic twist, issue me a visa, as a Pakistani, on my Canadian passport. I refused. I am proud of my Pakistani heritage, but I am a Canadian first and foremost.

Under visa rules adopted in 2008, individuals like me are subjected to an Indian version of the Nuremberg rules as applied by the Nazis to classify people as Jewish based on their ancestry. Under these rules, for the purposes of the Government of India, I am deemed to be Pakistani rather than Canadian.

In the meantime, I try to keep the brutal and troubling memories of Partition that my family endured from fading altogether. Maybe one day we will know more.

I

Ballet is not for Muslim Girls

Mariam, 1969

"There's a letter for you," said Mummy. She passed me the peanut butter just as the bread popped up out of the toaster. Peanut butter on toast was my favourite after-school snack and I was famished. I took a huge bite. My mouth full, I motioned with my hand for my mother to pass me my mail.

"Finish eating, then you can read it," she said. "I don't want you to get the envelope smeared and greasy with peanut butter! Here's your milk."

I wolfed down my food, choking and washing down the dry crust with the remaining milk in the glass. I almost tripped over my feet as I raced to put the plate and glass in the sink. Who could the letter be from? It was April 1968, and my tenth birthday was not for another six months. It couldn't be a birthday card.

Mummy picked up the letter from the table at the top of the stairs. She handed me the blue airmail envelope. It had a red Pakistani stamp. I looked at the return address – it was from my grandfather in Pakistan, my *Dada Abajee*. I smiled and held the letter tightly. He had finally replied! I had almost forgotten that I had written him.

Three months earlier, I asked my mother if I could write *Dada Abajee* a letter. Mummy wrote him every week using a stamped international aerogramme that she bought at the post office. She said yes. After she had filled up most of the thin blue paper with her small, neat handwriting, she called me to come to the kitchen.

"There you are, Mariam, I'm finished. I left this section for you." She pointed at the blank part.

"Are you ready?"

I had practiced my text in pencil on scrap paper. I carefully copied it onto the aerogramme using my new blue Bic pen. No mistakes! I smiled as I signed my name.

Mummy took the aerogramme and expertly folded it so it created its own envelope. She licked the three flaps and pressed them closed with her finger.

"Can I go and mail it now?" I said.

"Of course you can. But don't dawdle, you have home-work to do."

I ran to the red mailbox at the corner of our street, and I slid the thin envelope into the slot. Panting, I heard my letter drop softly onto the pile of mail that was already in the box. As I walked back to the house, I wondered how long it would be before *Dada Abajee* replied.

"Can you please open it for me?" I asked my mother, handing it to her. Expertly, she angled the pointed tip of the wood knife, shaped like a flying fish, under the flap and drew it quickly across to slit it. She gave me the opened envelope. I gingerly extracted a thin piece of paper and unfolded it. The letter was typed in black ink on my grandfather's letterhead. I had never seen anything like it.

I looked at the transparent sheet. I could see my hand through it. In the upper left-hand corner, in navy blue, bold, block capitals, was written "SIRAJUDDIN PAL, MA, LLB, Senior Advocate, Supreme Court of Pakistan." In the upper right-hand corner, below a five-digit phone number and the familiar address of the family home (and my grandfather's law office), 1 Fane Road, Lahore, the date was typed: March 19, 1968.

I bent my head to read:

> *My dear granddaughter Mariam,*
>
> *I was much delighted to read your letter and the remarks of your mother about your progress at the school. The answer to your question is simple, i.e., because your Papa is a Muslim and Islam does not encourage ballet for girls. I hope you can do without it; there is much scope for you in various branches of science.*
>
> *Love to you and to little Salma,*
> *Sirajuddin Pal*

My grandfather had signed in blue ink above his typed name.

With every word I read, I felt worse. My mother was waiting. "So, what did he say?"

Holding back tears, I handed her the flimsy paper. *Dada Abajee*, my last hope, had said no. I desperately wanted to take ballet lessons, but my father did not approve and neither did my grandfather. What would I do now? It never occurred to me that he would say no. I tried to understand *Dada Abajee's* suggestion that science was better than ballet even though it made no sense to me. We had done some fun things in science class, but ballet, with its pretty outfits and graceful gestures, was so much better! Moreover, I was baffled as to why Muslim girls could not learn ballet. Was there something bad about ballet that I didn't know about? I couldn't imagine what.

After dinner, in my bedroom, I refolded the letter, carefully following the original lines. I put it in the shoebox on my bookshelf where I kept birthday cards and postcards. The contents of my shoebox became part of a larger collection of old cards and letters that followed me as I grew up, left home, moved in and out of a series of apartments, and eventually lived abroad.

مریم

Four decades later, I decided to sort through my old letters. I lived in Asia. By now, my collection of correspondence had swelled to a dozen boxes, which had followed me around the world. I spent many evenings sorting through hundreds of envelopes, cards, and papers. One day, I found a folded piece of brittle paper wedged underneath the bottom flap of one of the boxes. It was a letter. It was not in an envelope, and it was written on a thin off-white paper that used to be called onionskin. I carefully unfolded it. The letter was from my grandfather in Pakistan. I sat and read his letter. I had completely forgotten that I had written to *Dada Abajee* and that he replied.

Reading his answer jolted me back to 1968, and to my pining to study ballet. Four decades later, I was initially astonished by the apparent insensitivity of my grandfather's response. How could science possibly compare to the romance of ballet for a young girl? Clearly *Dada Abajee* was a man with no sisters or daughters, I thought to myself, as I struggled to understand his reasoning. Later, it also occurred to me that he was not a typical Pakistani man; after all, he encouraged me to study science in an era when these were not traditional pursuits for women in either Canada or Pakistan.

I'm not sure if my *Dada Abajee* knew what ballet was. How could he have realized, sitting at his desk in Pakistan, what was involved in his nine-year-old granddaughter taking ballet lessons in Canada? I doubt that he ever attended a ballet recital in his life.

I did a little online research about ballet and Muslim girls. As I read the opinions written by male Muslim religious leaders on various websites, I learned that they considered ballet to be *haram*, or a forbidden activity, because unrelated males and females touch when they dance together. This is certainly true for professional dancers. Yet, as any Canadian who has ever been to a ballet recital of nine-year-old girls knows, little pre-pubescent ballerinas do not *pas de deux* with little boys. Such events are a flurry of shy little girls in pink leotards, tights, and tutus performing variations on the five positions, *arabesques*, and *pliés*. How could my *Dada Abajee* know this?

مریم

A book sparked my interest in ballet. On one of my regular Saturday morning trips to the library with my mother, the children's librarian came over to where I was standing, studying the bookshelves. Her name was Mrs. Powell. She wore pretty dresses and smelled of roses.

"Good morning, Mariam. Can I help you look?"

"I don't know which one to choose," I said.

"I have an idea. I'll be right back."

She swished by and I caught a whiff of roses. Seconds later, she was back beside me, a dog-eared pink hardcover book in hand. "I think you might like this one. It's very popular with a lot of girls your age."

The book was the first in the Sadler's Wells ballet series, "A Dream of Sadler's Wells." Its heroine is Fiona, a young orphan. Fiona had to move from London, where she studied ballet at Sadler's Wells, to Newcastle, where there was no ballet school. Fiona pined for London, especially for her ballet lessons.

Besotted with ballet, I soon devoured all fourteen books in the series. With Mrs. Powell's help, I also borrowed an instructtional book on ballet. Following the lessons carefully,

I taught myself the five positions. I practiced twice a day in the bathroom using the towel bar for support. I badgered my mother to buy me a new ballerina print bedspread from the Eaton's catalogue. I pestered my parents for a French provincial style dresser with a huge mirror because this is what I thought any aspiring ballerina should have. Eventually, I got both. But more than anything, I wanted to take ballet lessons.

Some of the girls at school took ballet lessons with Madame Lasalle every week after school in the gym. On Thursdays, they all brought their leotard, pink tights, and little ballet shoes to school in tote bags. When the bell rang, signaling the end of the day, they scampered into the girls' bathroom to change, giggling and talking. They emerged a few minutes later, a jumble of pinks and tutus, and ran down the corridor into the gym. How I wished I were one of them! Instead, I put on my coat, hopped onto my bike, and headed home.

"Please, Mummy, can I take ballet after school? It looks so nice! Pleeeeaassse?" Mummy looked at the piece of paper I had brought home from school. She frowned and said, "Expensive. Then there are also the shoes and other things to buy. I'll have to talk to your father. Okay?"

A couple of days later, while getting dressed for school, I overheard my parents talking. They were sitting at the kitchen table having their morning tea.

"Ballet? Why does she want to study ballet? No, I do not approve. I got dragged to a performance when I was in London – very silly! And those men in tights look ridiculous." Papa laughed, remembering what he had seen.

23

"All right, I'll tell her. Besides, all these afterschool activities are pricey!"

"That's right," said Papa, folding the newspaper. "Money doesn't grow on trees."

That day, after school, Mummy broke the news.

"I discussed it with your father, and he said no. Ballet lessons are expensive and there are special clothes and shoes to buy. You got a beautiful blue bike for your birthday. You can ride it around the neighbourhood after school." Mummy smiled. "Okay, my little chicken?"

"Okay," I mumbled as I went down the hall to my room. I picked up my book and pretended to read.

Why was it that I never got to do anything the other girls did? Since starting grade one, my parents hadn't allowed me to take after school activities like Scottish dancing, Brownies, or piano. Now ballet. I didn't really understand why. It was bad enough that I had a "funny" name; my lack of participation in any after school classes further branded me as different.

A day later, I walked by the gym on my way home from school. It was Thursday, ballet class day. Through the closed doors I heard the piano. Madame Lasalle, the ballet teacher, was shouting instructions. "*Les filles! Pliés! En barre!*" As I slowly walked by, I felt a hot tear slide down my cheek. It was all so unfair!

Then I had an idea. I decided to write my grandfather. My friend Karen's grandfather, who visited every winter from Saskatchewan, occasionally took her side against her strict parents. I was sure my far away grandfather would be my ally. Soon I would be joining the other girls on Thursdays for ballet lessons!

After I received the letter from *Dada Abajee*, my interest in ballet came to an abrupt end. I stopped practising the five positions in the bathroom. I finished the Sadler's Wells ballet series; there were new books about other places for me to discover. As the weeks and months went by, *Dada Abajee*, like the *arabesques* and *pliés* I used to rehearse, faded even more from my memory. The letter he wrote me about ballet lessons is the only one I ever received from him. Even though it evokes painful memories, I treasure it.

The Dégas dancers on my ballet bedspread pirouetted across my mattress for several years. Eventually, the colour faded with repeated washings and I remember that my thrifty mother cut it up into rags. When I was thirteen, I got a new orange chenille bedspread that was more appropriate for someone starting junior high in the early 1970s. The French provincial dresser with the big mirror remained in my old bedroom long after I left home. But one thing has not changed: I still love peanut butter.

2

The Dancer from Heera Mandi

Catherine at the wheel in Vehari, 1961.

D ada Abajee, my Pakistani grandfather, never answered the telephone. He stood in front of it watching it ring.

"Gafoor! Telephonnnne! *Jaldi! Jaldi!* Gafooooor!" he bellowed.

Gafoor, one of the family servants, came running, picked up the telephone, and said, in a perfect English accent, "Hellooo. *Salaam. Acha. Aik* minute please."

Gafoor passed the receiver to *Dada Abajee.*

"Hello? HELLO? Yes, *walaykum salaam* to you, too. Your name please? Vehari, you say? Speak louder please! I cannot understand what you are saying, my good sir. Hello, I said, HELLO?" *Dada Abajee* strained to understand the voice on the crackly line. He managed to catch several words: "Your son ... in Vehari ... married ... children." The line was dead. He hung up the heavy black telephone and sat staring at the spinning ceiling fan in disbelief.

"Izzmia!!" *Dada Abajee* roared, calling for his youngest son, my father. "I just received a very disturbing telephone call . . ."

It was the summer of 1961 in Lahore, Pakistan. Middle Uncle, one of my father's two older brothers, was soon to be wed. My grandparents had arranged his marriage, as was and is, the custom in Pakistan. Apparently, Middle Uncle had been holding out for what Pakistanis call a "love match" which is when you choose your own spouse. But at thirty-seven, his parents had waited long enough so they found him a suitable bride.

Middle Uncle was the District Magistrate in Vehari, a dusty southern Punjabi town. My grandparents and their eldest son, Big Uncle, and his family, lived in Lahore, two hundred miles north. The wedding was to take place later that summer, thus coinciding with a planned visit by my parents and I from Canada. I was three years old.

Two weeks before the wedding, a man telephoned *Dada Abajee*. He said he was calling from Vehari but refused to give his name. Middle Uncle, said the man, was already married to a Punjabi woman, and they had three children. There was more – the "wife" was said to be a former dancing girl (prostitute). *Dada Abajee* booked an emergency long-distance telephone call through the operator. Middle Uncle confessed. Uproar ensued at the family home.

The wedding festivities were cancelled. *Ammi Jee*, my grandmother, was humiliated and devastated. She cried non-stop and refused to leave the house. A broken engagement was a rare and scandalous occurrence in 1960s Lahore – and would be viewed as such even now. Which was worse – that Middle Uncle had a Punjabi wife, or that she was a dancing girl? Both revelations sent shockwaves through the whole clan.

My Pakistani family is ethnically Kashmiri. Residents of the Punjab for generations, they had always married within the Kashmiri community. My father's marriage to my Canadian mother was the first deviation from this long-standing tradition that anyone could recall. Her status as a foreigner and the family's affection for her seemed to have compensated for her lack of Kashmiri-ness.

My mother – Mummy – and *Ammi Jee* had become good friends two years earlier when Papa brought his new wife and nine-month-old daughter to Lahore for the first time. It didn't matter that the two women didn't share a common language. They bonded trying to keep me healthy and cool in the oppressive and debilitating heat of a scorching Lahore summer.

Mummy intuitively understood the depth of *Ammi Jee's* despair over Middle Uncle's situation. Looking at her husband she said, "*Izzmia*, why don't you go there and find out for yourself what is going on? Go to Vehari and visit him. Maybe he'll open up to you."

She sat down on the *charpai* beside him. "After all, we travelled all the way from Canada. It's normal to want to visit your elder brother. He'd be thrilled to see how much Mariam has grown."

"You're right. I'll check if the car is available," replied Papa.

A plan was made – the three of us would travel from Lahore to Vehari. At the last minute, *Dada Abajee* decided to join us for the trip.

Family driver at the wheel, we headed south on the Multan Road, an old highway built by the Mughals in the sixteenth century and upgraded by the British. Air-conditioned cars were rare in Pakistan in 1961. Although we left at dawn, the trip took several hours and once the sun was up it beat down on us mercilessly. By the time our party reached Vehari, the temperature must have been in the mid-forties, suffocating and dry.

A thoroughly unremarkable place, Vehari is one of dozens of towns created in the desert of southern Punjab a hundred years ago when the British built the largest irrigation canal system in the world. As people moved to the irrigated areas, settlements soon followed.

There was no hotel in Vehari, so Papa rented a nearby government guesthouse for the night. A British colonial relic, the houses are fully furnished, including a cook. My father's black-and-white photographs, taken in the guesthouse garden, show a dry, dusty yard with a few scraggly trees desperate for the August monsoon. In one photo my mother balances me on her lap. I look hot and unhappy.

Middle Uncle and his wife, Shamshad, came to the guesthouse. She stares, pretty and unsmiling, directly at the camera, cradling a newborn baby girl whose name was Amber. Standing beside her, Middle Uncle looks awkward, young, and handsome.

Later, the family learned that there were also two boys, Asad and Wasid, both of whose fathers were unknown. In a highly patriarchal society like Pakistan, not knowing one's father smacks of *sharm*, or shame. Where did they come from?

The mission to Vehari was a failure. Middle Uncle wouldn't talk. The two brothers spoke privately, but as Papa said to me years later, "I couldn't get through to him." The four of us headed back to Lahore. Middle Uncle's secret – why he married a dancing girl – remained a mystery. The wedding was definitely off.

Middle Uncle's jilted fiancée married someone else.

After Vehari, Middle Uncle's relationships with the rest of the family were never the same. The secret loomed large. Big Uncle broke all ties with his younger brother, who continued to work in rural Punjab. The two brothers occasionally ran into each other when visiting their father. Middle Uncle's family and Big Uncle's family, who lived in their own house located across the back lawn from *Dada Abajee*, had nothing to do with each other. *Dada Abajee*, in letters written to Mummy, regularly gave news of Middle Uncle but never mentioned Shamshad or the children.

On a trip to Pakistan with my father when I was eighteen, I asked Papa about Middle Uncle and his family. He told me that Shamshad had been born into a house of dancers in

Heera Mandi, Lahore's red-light district. It was no secret that Middle Uncle had been a regular there for years, spending countless evenings drinking scotch and listening to *ghazals* in the company of dancing girls. Fate had been kind to Shamshad when she entered into a liaison with my dapper Middle Uncle. A gentleman, he probably took her at her word when she claimed that he was Amber's father. Papa did not tell me how he knew so much about Shamshad, nor did I ask.

Twelve years after the Vehari trip, my *Dada Abajee* called Middle Uncle who was, by then, a judge posted to Lyallpur, a big Punjabi cotton-milling town. *Dada Abajee* pleaded with his son, "I am all alone. Your brother has moved to a new house. You must come home. I am old. I want to stay in my house. And yes, you can bring that woman and her children." Middle Uncle, shocked by how frail his father sounded, agreed to come home.

Middle Uncle had not lived in Lahore for many years. Overnight, he went from black sheep to dutiful son. He and his family settled into *Dada Abajee's* house and nursed my grandfather through his dying days. After his death in 1975, Middle Uncle's family continued to live in the family home. Respectable marriages were arranged for the two boys. Nobody knows if they were legally adopted. Following Pakistani tradition, they and their offspring use Middle Uncle's first name as their surname. An annex was built for the extended families.

Fifteen years after the Vehari trip, Big Uncle and my father stopped speaking to each other. Of course it was about their inheritance; in Pakistan it always is. Papa

31

claimed Big Uncle had received what Papa liked to call "the lion's share" of my grandfather's property. Papa and Middle Uncle decided to challenge the will. Their case went nowhere for years. Then Papa discovered that it was Middle Uncle's delaying tactics, not the Pakistani bureaucracy, that explained the slow progress in the case. Now none of the three brothers were talking to each other.

After Big Uncle and Papa's relationship soured, family visits changed. We no longer visited with Big Uncle's family. Instead, we spent time with Middle Uncle and his family.

By the late 1970s, nearly three decades after Vehari, Shamshad looked very different from the pretty young woman in the 1961 photos. Now portly and shrill with orange hennaed hair and teeth stained brown from chewing *paan* (betel nut), she held court on the veranda, dragging on a Wills unfiltered cigarette and sitting with her legs apart like an American football player while she ordered the servants around. On one of my trips to Lahore in the '80s, she extracted a framed studio portrait of herself from an old, battered metal trunk. The black-and-white photo showed an arresting face, heavily made up and framed by gaudy jewellery in the exaggerated style of a 1950s Bollywood siren.

My father could only tolerate Shamshad in small doses. She only cooked Punjabi food and knew none of the Kashmiri dishes that he pined for. In the rare private moments that we would have on our Pakistan trips my Papa would shake his head and ask me, "What does my brother see in her?"

Middle Uncle died first. A trained lawyer, he did not leave a will. His survivors sued my father in Pakistani court, claiming ownership rights of the house. A settlement was reached out of court. After telling me this on the phone, Papa said, "I forbid you to go to Middle Uncle's house."

"What?" I said, shocked. "How old do you think I am, five? I will do what I want."

At the time, in my early forties, I was frequently in Pakistan for work, and I continued to visit Middle Uncle's family. "Mum's the word," I said – and they agreed. But somehow Papa found out. Inheritance disputes are cruel and painful. I chose not to provoke Papa any further. I decided to keep everyone at arms'-length until after my father died in 2013, fifty years after the Vehari trip. Now we have all found each other on Facebook and WhatsApp. Middle Uncle and Big Uncle's children, grandchildren, and great-grandchildren have never met but often relatives from both sides react to one of my Facebook posts or Instagram photos.

Nearly four decades after the Vehari visit, Big Uncle called Papa from Pakistan in the middle of the night. He was terminally ill. Before he died in 2000, Big Uncle, a prominent lawyer and former High Court judge, told Papa that he had "made it his business" to find out the truth about his younger brother. Big Uncle claimed to have discovered proof that Amber was not Middle Uncle's biological daughter but also that he and Shamshad never married.

Sixty years later, so many questions remain unanswered. How did Middle Uncle meet Shamshad? Was she really from *Heera Mandi*? Was Middle Uncle blackmailed? Who was the mystery caller? How did the mystery caller know so much about Middle Uncle's private life? Some family members have even hinted darkly that perhaps he was involved in some type of criminal activity and was forced to marry Shamshad. Others say they were never married. My father disagreed; he adhered to the gallant gentleman theory.

The secret of Middle Uncle and why or if he married the dancing girl is now tightly woven into the family fabric. Both Big Uncle and Middle Uncle's families have erased each other from their family trees. Middle Uncle's secret created a rift between the two older brothers that was never repaired. The secret's dividing knife pierces through the second and third generations and will soon slice through a fourth. I am the only person in the family who communicates with both sides.

Six decades after the Vehari visit, and a quarter-century after his death, Middle Uncle's secret life remains a sensitive subject with some of Big Uncle's family. The story that I find so fascinating is a source of deep embarrassment to them, whether they live in Pakistan, the USA, or England. One cousin cannot bear to hear mention of Middle Uncle because she is so ashamed that she is related to him. Another does not hide her disgust – pointing out to me "his so-called children enjoy the privilege of carrying the family name when they are not blood relatives." They are puzzled as to why I cannot share their shame. I cannot. All I see is sadness. And the power of a secret to tear family ties forever.

3

Mar-tea-ni Time!

Mariam, 1984

Big Uncle was coming to visit from Pakistan! The whole house was in a tizzy as preparations swung into high gear. My younger sister moved into my room, there were extra towels in the bathroom, a fifth chair at the dining room table, and special meals planned. Big Uncle, my father's eldest brother, would arrive in Victoria on a Monday in September 1970.

Only two days to go, I thought as I sat at my bedroom desk struggling to write a grade seven essay about Tasmania. It was hard to concentrate with all the excitement. I heard the clatter as my mother took out the good china and stacked it on the kitchen counter. My father's animated voice floated down the hallway into my room.

"We can't leave all this bar stuff out in plain view," said Papa.

I knew he was talking about five or six bottles (sherry, scotch, gin, vermouth, brandy) clustered in a far corner of the kitchen counter, out of the way but within easy reach. They had always been there.

"Why not?" said Mummy. "I'm not Muslim. Your big brother shouldn't have a problem with me drinking. Come on now, you're a grown man. What are you so nervous about?"

Papa didn't reply. I could hear him moving something. Clink. Clink. Glass against glass. Then I heard his voice, muffled by the cupboard.

"Here, I've made some room underneath the kitchen sink. Behind the cleaning supplies. It's perfect!"

So the booze was banished behind the bleach, ammonia, and other poisons, but the bottles would be easily accessible in case Papa needed an emergency martini during Big Uncle's five-day visit.

Papa was a creature of habit. His days opened with morning tea and closed with nightly martinis (with an olive). He only broke the martini tradition when he visited his home country, Pakistan, whose name literally translates as "land of the pure." It is also a place where Muslims cannot legally purchase alcohol, a prohibition that extends up to Pakistani airspace. After one especially long, gin-free family visit, Papa ordered a martini as soon as the Swissair pilot announced that our plane was out of Pakistani skies.

"Cheers," he said to me in a low growl, raising his glass to the ceiling. "To the land of the pure."

Papa was the youngest of three brothers. Except for my father, they all lived in Lahore, Pakistan. Their father, my grandfather *Dada Abajee*, was a devout Muslim. He had a small dark callous on his forehead, earned during a lifetime of kneeling and touching his head to the ground in prayer five times daily. *Dada Abajee* never drank or smoked and expected the same of his sons. Big Uncle, the eldest son and religious, followed in his father's footsteps by becoming a lawyer and marrying the cousin chosen for him. Middle Uncle, also a lawyer, was not especially devout. As a young man, he spent evenings drinking scotch, listening to music, and watching dancing girls in Lahore's red-light district. He did not marry the woman selected for him. Papa was somewhere in the middle. He had discovered beer as a student in London and refused to marry a woman picked by his parents because he wanted to get to know his future wife. Papa defined himself as a "statistical Muslim" which basically meant he was secular.

"Now, girls, while your uncle is visiting, a few things will be different around here," said Papa sternly. "We're putting all these bottles away. Your uncle doesn't like people to drink, and your mother and I don't want him to get upset."

"In Pakistan they do things differently," he continued. "So let's not talk about how you sometimes have a little bit of wine in your water at your birthday and things like that. Okay?"

"Okay," I replied. But I was confused. If people in Pakistan don't drink martinis and my father was from there, then why did he drink martinis?

Although I was supposed to be a Muslim, my knowledge of Islam was negligible. Just a few weeks before Big Uncle's visit, my father had announced that he would start weekly lessons on Islam on Sunday mornings in September. I liked to call it Sunday School for Muslims. As my education had just started, we had not yet dealt with alcohol. Needless to say, my father moved this subject forward on the curriculum.

Papa did not have the typical right versus wrong view of drinking alcohol that most Pakistanis espouse. His interpretation was that Islam does not ban alcohol but rather counselled restraint. In Papa's opinion the rigid ban on drinking had become part of Islamic doctrine thanks to overly literal translations and understandings of the Koran. My father impressed on me that alcohol itself was not the problem but that, like any vice, it should be taken in moderation. He was satisfied that his nightly martini fell within these guidelines.

When I wrote my father's obituary, I struggled to include some personal details. I was writing around the cocktail hour, so I included a reference to his nightly martini. His morning tea ritual did not even occur to me. Later, I thought that he wouldn't have approved of my sharing this private detail with the world. He would not have wanted the people who admired his academic work on Islam and economics to know that he drank. Decades after Papa left Pakistan, the taboo stayed with him. His religious upbringing and his father's strict rules haunted him. It was as if he knew he was doing something wrong, despite all of his bravado and justifications.

I never thought to ask my father why, if he was so confident that his reading of the Koran was correct, he was adamant that Big Uncle not know that he drank regularly. Was he afraid of what he might say? Was he worried that his eldest brother would tell their father? Perhaps Papa suspected that his father, a scholarly man, would have ripped his smooth justification to shreds. I think he wisely decided not to flaunt his acceptance of alcohol and cause tension during such a short visit. Instead, they consumed tea. There was always tea, lots of tea.

Tea is the beverage that I associate with Pakistan. Big Uncle, like most Pakistanis, loved his tea. Brewed in a pot, served in proper teacups with saucers, astounding amounts of sugar, and plenty of hot milk. Pakistani tea is so strong that it is almost coffee black.

Tea, or *chai*, is everywhere in Pakistan. Served in clear glasses with buffalo milk and lots of sugar, it can be purchased from roadside stalls run by *chai wallahs*. Tea is offered to visitors, clients, and colleagues at all times of the day or night. Tea lubricates any and all social situations, from buying carpets and meeting with government officials, to getting together with friends. Pakistanis meet for tea the way Canadians bond over a Labatt Blue or a double-double from Tim Hortons. I learned that in government meetings in Pakistan, the higher-ranking the person you are meeting, the finer the tea set and the better the biscuits that accompany it. And if you aren't offered tea, well, you just know something is wrong.

Every morning of his visit, Big Uncle joined my parents for morning tea. It was the only time I could ever remember that morning tea was taken in the living room. The three of them would sit and reminisce for an hour or so. My mother brought out the china teacups and saucers and heated the milk so that the temperature of the tea remained blistering hot.

My parents always began the day with a pot of tea. They used loose tea – never teabags. Sitting at the kitchen table they would discuss the day ahead while CBC voices prattled in the background. Papa took his morning tea with milk and sugar and Mummy took hers just with milk. As children, on Sundays my sister and I were allowed some milky tea in little espresso cups. After my mother died, my father continued the morning tea tradition for twenty-six years. When I lived abroad and came home to visit, I would join him very early, struggling with jet lag. It was a quiet time for us to catch up. Four days before he died, my last visit with my father was over a cup of tea. Although I have shared many drinks with my father, it is the times we drank tea together, rather than martini time, that I remember fondly.

I enjoy a good cup of tea, and still prefer to brew it like my parents did. But unlike them, I never acquired the morning tea habit. Tea is lovely but at the start of my day it's coffee that I crave. Eli, my husband, is a dedicated tea drinker who consumes two cups of tea in the morning and one after lunch and dinner. He uses loose tea, never teabags, and is partial to delicate floral teacups.

On our first date, Eli ordered a dry martini with engineering precision – Bombay Sapphire gin, no ice shards in the glass, a whisper of vermouth and a twist of citrus.

I don't care for martinis. I prefer one of the European aperitifs like Campari or Dubonnet. And alcohol is not a deal-breaker for me, especially in a "dry" country like Pakistan. I certainly relish a cocktail, but not being able to quaff a cold beer or sip on an icy martini at the end of a hot day doesn't irritate me the way it seemed to get under my father's skin. For Papa, the consumption of alcohol was a declaration of freedom.

The first time they met, Eli and Papa drank tea together. The second time, they had martinis. My Montréal-born, Jewish husband and his Pakistani-Canadian father-in-law had many cultural differences. Lubricated by tea, martinis, and their love for me, they found common ground.

مریم

Big Uncle's visit was the first time that I realized that some people, including Big Uncle and my grandfather, considered drinking alcohol a sin. I had been to Pakistan just two years before, as a ten-year-old, but I hadn't noticed whether my father drank alcohol or not. I did have a vivid memory of drinking brilliant orange Fantas, one after another, until I got sick.

Unsurprisingly, the 1977 prohibition against Muslims buying alcohol in Pakistan created a thriving black market. A remarkable selection of beer, spirits, and wines became available for home delivery throughout the country with just a telephone call. Middle Uncle lived in the family home with my *Dada Abajee* and cared for his aging father. After my grandfather died in 1975, Middle Uncle was finally free to have a drink at home. Two years later he celebrated his younger brother's visit from Canada by procuring a good bottle of imported Scotch whiskey. Ironically, the purchase and consumption of alcohol by Muslims had been banned a few months earlier. The bottle occupied a place of honour during long evenings spent talking with old friends. Papa found their get-togethers taxing because Pakistanis drink to get drunk and then eat. He was used to Western ways: a cocktail before, and wine with dinner.

As a young woman at age eighteen and again at twenty-one, I accompanied Papa on trips to Pakistan. I often spent entire evenings watching a group of grown men, except Papa, get increasingly drunk. The talk would become livelier as the evening wore on. Only one or two of my father's friends attempted to engage me in conversation. Papa and Middle Uncle both offered me some scotch, which I refused. I had yet to develop a taste for it.

One day towards the end of Big Uncle's visit, my father came home from work earlier than usual. Sitting in the kitchen over yet another cup of tea, I was gamely trying to explain my passion for the Beatles to Big Uncle. He didn't approve of the giant George Harrison poster on the wall above my bed that I had saved up my allowance to buy. I stood up and started to leave the kitchen. My father stopped me.

"Well, Mariam," said my father. He smiled at me in a way that made me know something was going on. "Before it gets dark why don't you take your uncle on a walk? You can show him your favourite beach."

"Oh, yes, what a great idea!" said Big Uncle, smiling at me.

This seemed odd. Why, all of a sudden, did Papa want me to take Big Uncle to the beach? We had already been there!

"I don't feel like it, Papa," I moaned. "I'm tired. School was really hard today. Those horrible new teachers made us go for a huge, long run in P.E."

"All the more reason for you to stretch your legs," Papa said. "So you won't be sore tomorrow. Come on. It'll be dark soon."

Before I knew it my mother and father hustled us out the door. My mother smiled. "Have a nice walk!" Wham! The door slammed behind us. My anger disappeared when, seconds later, I realized what was going on. My father wanted to unwind with a martini. I kept my thoughts to myself as we walked to the end of the driveway. When Big Uncle said, "Which way do we turn?" I replied, "Go to the right," because I knew it was the longer way to the beach.

After five days Big Uncle left. We all went to the airport to see him off. Standing behind the chain-link fence that separated us from the tarmac I waved good-bye and as I did, I turned to look at Papa. A single tear ran down his cheek. It was the first time I had ever seen him cry. We watched the plane until it disappeared into the horizon.

Life in our house returned to normal. The extra towel and chair were taken away and I had my bedroom back. That evening I heard the familiar slide of the bottles on the counter and the ice cube tray cracking as Papa made his nightly martini.

4

The Most Bee-oo-tee-ful
Dress in the World

Mariam, Lahore, 1968

"The tailor is here!" screamed my cousin. I charged after her into the courtyard of my grandfather's house in Lahore, Pakistan. A tall, skinny man stood there, talking to my aunt. He balanced a black sewing machine on his right shoulder. A bag hung from his left. Deftly, he lowered his body and in one fluid movement he slid the hand-operated Singer from his shoulder onto the lawn.

My cousin and I, both ten years old, watched, intrigued, as he set up his *atelier* underneath one of the trees. My aunt brought a small low table from the house and soon it was stacked with shiny pieces of satin in tones of ruby, sapphire, and topaz. Carefully, the tailor extracted an enormous pair of scissors, a battered box of pins, a frayed measuring tape, and some chalk out of his cloth bag and put them on the table. The tailor sat on the grass and surveyed the temporary workshop where he would sew the family's *shalwar kameezes* for the upcoming *Eid* celebrations.

The typical dress worn by girls and women in Pakistan, the *shalwar kameez* (or simply *shalwar* for short) consists of a knee-length tunic (the *kameez*) worn over a pair of loose pants gathered at the waist (the *shalwar*). A matching diaphanous scarf, usually made out of chiffon, called the *dupatta*, completes the ensemble.

In December 1968, Papa and I were visiting Lahore for the first time since I was a baby.

The day before the tailor arrived, I went shopping in the bazaar with my father, aunt, and cousins. We purchased some red satin and brilliant gold trim for my outfit. My father declared the cloth "gaudy," but I loved it. I was excited and wrote about my new outfit in my travel diary: "December 19, 1968, 9:50 a.m. I am getting a new *shalwar kameez* for *Eid*. It is red with gold trimmings." Wearing red satin seemed very Christmassy to me and more exotic than the pink dress with the white scalloped collar that I wore to birthday parties in Canada.

Two months earlier, I took a sewing course after school and had learned basic stitches. I was fascinated by the

Lahore tailor's hand-cranked sewing machine. Not needing electricity, it could be used anywhere. This seemed very practical to me. The tailor worked, cross-legged, underneath the tree for several days. I loved watching him turn the wheel of the machine with his right hand while he fed the fabric under the needle with the other. When he was finished, the pile of cloth had been transformed into a shimmering stack of *shalwars*.

My aunt took me to the Bata shoe store to buy a pair of black Mary-Jane-style shoes. On the first day of *Eid*, my teenage cousin braided a gold tassel into my waist-long hair. I still have the tassel. I keep it in a trunk filled with items to which I have a sentimental attachment – my baby shoes, my teddy bear, and an old jewellery box.

I loved my red satin *shalwar kameez* and wanted to wear it every day. In a photograph taken during the trip I squint into the camera, dorky and bewildered, wearing my gaudy red outfit and showing off my tasselled braid.

When I returned to Canada it was the middle of winter, so my mother put my red satin *shalwar* away. A year later, I tried it on for *Eid*. I had grown and it was too small for me. Disappointed, I wore the gold trimmed *dupatta* over my party dress. After my father died, I found it in a big trunk of old clothes. It was still red and shiny, decades later.

At age eighteen, I returned to Pakistan with my father for the first time since I was ten. I had just finished my first year of university. Instead of going to Pakistan, I wanted to stay in Canada and get a summer job so that I could buy the contact lenses my father refused to pay for. I hated wearing glasses and was convinced that they made me look like a librarian, not the stylish person I wanted to be. I was insecure about my appearance and not always sure what suited me. Choosing my clothes was an important part of my identity and a way of asserting my independence. But in Pakistan my choices were taken away from me.

"Mariam, you are a young woman now and need to dress modestly once we arrive in Pakistan. How about wearing long loose tops and pants?"

"But Papa, I don't wear long loose tops and pants. I hate loose tops. Am I supposed to look like a sack of potatoes?"

"If you insist on wearing jeans and t-shirts you'll really stand out. Men will stare at you. You'll look even more like a *firunghi* (foreigner)."

I knew my father was right. Inside I seethed with frustration. What I wore was very important to me and I was just finding my style. I did not understand the Pakistani notion of modesty. It seemed to me that women were supposed to be invisible. I was used to options when it came to clothing – pants, skirts, and dresses. The notion of only dressing within the narrow parameters of the *shalwar* bothered me. After some thought and discussion with my mother, I decided to wear cotton pants underneath summer dresses. While these awkward ensembles met the modesty threshold, I felt dowdy and ridiculous. I longed for my snazzy fitted jeans, clogs, and Marilyn Monroe t-shirt.

After my arrival in Lahore, my aunt and my cousin embarked on a campaign to get me into *shalwar kameezes*.

"Oh, Mariam," they gushed, "you must wear the *shalwar*. It is the most bee-oo-tee-ful dress in the world. So versatile. Look at you in the picture." They proudly showed me the picture from my previous trip where ten-year-old me, in ugly cat-eye glasses and a braid down my back wears the red satin *shalwar*. In hindsight, I had to agree with my father about the fabric – it was pretty awful.

"See how beautiful you look!" they said as I cringed, wondering how they could think of comparing me to a child.

The battle to get me into *shalwars* went into high gear. My cousins bought me several ready-made outfits in colours and prints that they hoped I would like and which they assured me would look gorgeous. Knowing how hard they were trying, I put them on but in the end, I rejected them all; the colour wasn't right, the print was ugly, or the size was wrong. I felt awkward wearing a *shalwar*, like I was treading water in all the fabric. It just wasn't me. I couldn't get the hang of the flimsy chiffon *dupatta*, which usually measures a metre wide and two metres long. My *dupattas* got caught in doors, skewered with a seat belt, or sailed off my shoulders in the Anarkali bazaar.

One afternoon a pudgy American woman, wearing an especially unattractive *shalwar* in a shade that used to be called puce, came to visit. Middle Uncle had mentioned her as an example of a Western woman who had completely adapted to Pakistani dress. She told me she could never wear anything else, exclaiming, "It was like wearing pajamas all day long!" Good for you, I thought to myself, as I mentally counted down the days until I would be back in my Canadian clothes.

I resented being told what to wear. *Shalwars* made me feel frumpy and shapeless, not beautiful and exotic. I felt lost in the baggy pants and the long tunic and my body felt trapped inside a garment that did not tell the world who I was.

As I got dressed in the hotel room in Karachi for my flight home, the girl in the mirror looked like me for the first time since arriving in Pakistan. I strode onto the chilled Swissair jet bound for Zurich, wearing my jeans and a t-shirt tucked into the waistband. Buckling my seat belt, I took a deep breath as I leaned back into my seat. I was going home.

مریم

Seven years later, as a graduate student, I was hired to work with a Canadian team in rural Pakistan. My work, studying female poverty, would take me to villages in the month of May when temperatures in southern Punjab can shoot up to forty-six degrees Centigrade or more.

"But dear," said my mother, knowing how much I detested the *shalwar*, "you will be going to villages in the hottest month of the year. What will you wear?"

I discussed the clothing issue with my father. He suggested that I could have some tunics and loose pants made for me in Lahore – he called it an "east meets west" style. Although my aversion to the *shalwar* was strong, I also realized that to do field work I had to be dressed for my own comfort. Not only was it hot, but I would probably be sitting on the ground interviewing women and needed to be able to sit without showing my legs. I also needed to blend in – my mere presence would attract attention but the more "normal" I looked, the easier it would be for me to do my work. I decided to wear *shalwars*.

My father explained the situation in a letter to my Middle Uncle in Lahore. In his reply, Middle Uncle suggested the family tailor could sew me several outfits in the style known as "PIA pajamas," after the national airline of Pakistan (Pakistan International Airlines), whose hip stewardesses wore a slim-fitting *shalwar* styled by the French fashion designer Pierre Cardin. I was impressed by his fashion knowledge and agreed with his suggestion.

Several weeks later, I disembarked from the London to Islamabad flight. I wore slim, pale green vintage slacks, a tailored red-and-white-striped cotton hip-length tunic, and the red patent pumps that I bought with my first paycheque (I could not bear to leave them at home). My outfit was a more stylish twist on the dress and pants pairings I had worn when I was nineteen. I was covered but not draped with fabric. My male cousin, sent to pick me up at the airport and accompany me on the one-hour flight to Lahore, looked at my outfit with astonishment. In halting English, he managed to tell me that once we arrived in Lahore his wife would buy me "bee-oo-ti-full" *shalwars*. I cringed inside and smiled at him sweetly. "Yes, of course."

Several days later, the family tailor came to Middle Uncle's house (where I was staying for a week before my work started). I ordered three *shalwars*, all in solid-coloured Egyptian cotton purchased from the bazaar: pale pink, peach, and mauve. In the brutal heat of the Pakistani summer, the sorbet colours felt cool against my hot skin. No ugly prints and absolutely no *dupattas*, I insisted, as my cousin translated for the tailor.

Baffled by my style choices as well as by my adamant refusal to order matching *dupattas*, the tailor bashfully took my measurements and returned to his shop where he now had an electric sewing machine. A few days later, he delivered my clothes. I wrote home to my parents, "they turned out pretty sharp." Wearing them, I felt comfortable and moderately stylish as I traveled from village to village.

مریم

In Montréal, I consigned my *shalwars* to the back of my closet. Late one particularly hot and muggy August night, having run out of clean and comfortable clothing, I slipped on one of my *shalwars* while doing several loads of laundry. I didn't think to change when I darted out of my downtown apartment building to the corner store for some cherry Coke.

As *salaam a lai kum* (Hello) was all that I understood as a Pakistani man spoke to me in Urdu from the sidewalk. Seeing the lack of comprehension on my face, he switched into English. "What are you doing out alone, late at night?" He wore a white, male version of a *shalwar kameez* and from his beard and skullcap, I identified him as being religious. I didn't answer and kept walking. "So immodest. Such thin fabric and no *dupatta!*" he shouted after me. Grabbing the door of the dépanneur, I pulled it open and said, "We're in Canada," in a loud voice as I went into the store, slamming the door behind me. The clerk watched me curiously as I strolled slowly down the aisles and waited until the coast was clear before heading home with my drink. Soon after, I buried my sorbet-hued *shalwars* in a bag I donated to charity. I never walked the streets of Montréal in one again.

مریم

O ver the next two decades, my work in international development took me to Pakistan frequently. Traveling extensively throughout the country I became comfortable with the local culture, society, and food. Along the way, I improved my Urdu, got to know my family in Lahore, made my own friends and wore slim-fitting *shalwar kameezes* as well as the more traditional loose ones. I still don't agree that the *shalwar kameez* is the most "bee-oo-tee-ful" dress for women, but I came to appreciate its form and function. I learned about the variations in *shalwar* style, about tight *chooridar* pants and slim-fitting tops. I purchased *shalwars* made of exquisite silks at designer boutiques and attended fashion shows where the flexibility and versatility of the Pakistani national dress was praised. I remained unconvinced.

I also discovered the *sari*, a form of dress that is popular in India and worn by Pakistani women for special occasions. I learned how to put one on and brought two *saris* home to Canada where I would sometimes wear them to formal parties. My family in Pakistan was puzzled by my admiration of this garment, insisting that the *shalwar kameez* was the more practical and modest, not to mention beautiful, garment.

One day, I was out shopping in Lahore with my cousin when she gestured at some women in the distance. They were wearing *shalwars*, and *dupattas* on their heads. To my eye there was nothing special about them. But my cousin told me that they were foreign women – *firunghis*. I asked her how she could tell, and she said that foreign women were easy to spot by their walk, the way they held their head high, and how they looked you right in the eye.

Surprised by her response, I asked her if the fact that they were wearing traditional dress made any difference. "Oh, no," she said, and her husband nodded in agreement. "You can spot a foreign woman a mile away." As we walked by the women I wondered: what was the point of me wearing a *shalwar* if I was so visible as a foreigner anyway? Why had I even bothered?

Twenty-five years after the visit where I wore those clumsy dress and pants ensembles, I was in Pakistan as part of a team designing a drought relief project. I needed to make an unscheduled three-day visit to a rural area. I arranged to borrow several *shalwars* from a friend. The exquisite cotton lawn fabric of her lemon yellow-and-white outfit billowed and swirled around me as I walked. I wore the *dupatta* and managed to keep it on. Just like I did when I was eighteen, I felt lost in the garment and overpowered by the volume of the fabric. But now it was different. Nobody told me that I had to wear it; I chose to.

I knew who I was: a Canadian woman, of Pakistani heritage, but also an economist working at an international organization. I had grown into a woman confident of her own unique style and identity. The *shalwar* was merely a uniform for work.

A group of local officials were sent to greet the lemon-*shalwar*ed me in the lobby of the hotel where I was staying with my team. They didn't offer to shake my hand but acknowledged me with a polite and respectful nod of the head. By then I knew that not shaking a woman's hand is a sign of respect shown to Pakistani women. One of them said some words in Urdu. When I replied in fluent Canadian English they were clearly taken aback. Smiling, the senior official said, "Sorry madam, I thought you were a Pakistani. You don't look at all like a *firunghi*."

5
SAR-whaaaaat?!

Mariam, 1978

I spun the revolving rack of miniature license plates around as my eyes scanned the names. I whispered to myself, "Mary Ann, Marion, Marilyn." No Mariam. I turned to my mother.

"Mummy, why did you give me such a weird name? It's not on the rack. And everybody gets it wrong all the time." I scowled.

She smiled and said softly, "You have a special name, dear. People don't say your name wrong on purpose – they just don't know any better or don't listen carefully. You shouldn't get so upset."

Mummy gently steered me towards the other side of the shop. "Come on, look at these lovely pink streamers – how about we buy a pair for your bike?"

Trudging behind my mother, I cast a forlorn backward glance at the rack. I felt left out. Why wasn't my name there? I craved a keychain, a card, a box of pencils – anything that had my name on it.

Although I never got a personalized license plate for my bike, eventually I grew to love my name. No longer pining for a name on the rack, now I feel sad for the Mary Anns and Marilyns of this world. They may be able to buy a personalized post-it note, but their name is not unique like mine. While as a child I wanted to belong, as an adult I revel in being different.

Mariam

I grew up in Victoria in the 1960s and 1970s, a professor's daughter. When my sophisticated parents arrived there from Montréal in 1961, there were, according to my mother, only two types of cheese available: cottage and cheddar. A fitting metaphor – Victoria was a relatively homogeneous Anglo-Saxon community where people had predictable names that everyone knew how to spell and pronounce. Except for mine.

My first name stood out amongst the Julies and Lorraines with whom I attended primary and elementary school. Incredibly, the principal of my school persisted in calling me Marilyn for seven years. When I won the Citizenship award in grade seven, my name was engraved on the cup as "Miriam"! Nobody thought to check the records to make sure that they had spelled my name properly. Some of my parents' friends, despite my mother's diplomatic and gentle corrections, persisted in calling me "Marian" or "Miriam." I gave up trying to correct them years ago.

In my opinion, "Mariam" is not such a difficult name. "Mariam" is the Arabic form of Mary and equivalent to the French "Marie," the Italian or Spanish "Maria," or the Hebrew "Miriam." On this basis alone, my parents thought that "Mariam" was a good and relatively easy first name because it was a form of Mary, arguably one of the world's most popular female names. In the Middle East and in Pakistan it is often spelled "Maryam." Fearing that people would try to shorten my name to "Mary" my parents changed the "y" to an "i." In hindsight, my parents were right in changing the spelling – while my name has been mangled and twisted into many different variations, I have never been called "Mary."

The proper pronunciation of my name is based on the Arabic spelling. Arabic and English are very different; Arabic words are formed from consonants with vowel sounds added through punctuation marks. Consequently, it can be challenging to transcribe an Arabic word into English letters. While my name is pronounced with a longer, softer "a" in English, "Maariam," the Arabic pronunciation is a sharper "Mar-yum." The tongue moves from an 'm' sound to an 'r' then to a 'yum.' This is how my Pakistani father always said my name. My Canadian mother, whose first language was Polish but who spoke perfect English, was never able to say my name properly. Try as she might, she could never move her Ontario tongue from the "ma" to the "r" to the "yum" sound. She developed her own unique pronunciation. She added a syllable in the middle that resulted in "Maaddium." She diligently taught her family and friends this pronunciation and to this day, her siblings, my aunts and uncles, all pronounce my name like my mother did. My mother died in 1987 and sometimes it feels a little eerie when I pick up the phone and hear my aunt pronouncing my name just as my mother used to.

When I was ten years old, my family moved back to Montréal for a year while Papa took a sabbatical. One of my most satisfying memories was that nobody had any trouble with my name. I was astonished to get my report card on which all of my teachers had spelled my name correctly! A Jewish girl in my class named Merle explained to me my name was similar to the Hebrew "Miriam." It was a powerful gesture of acceptance that I had never experienced in Victoria. At the end of the year, I was sad to go back to Victoria where my grade six teacher, the sallow and sour Miss Constance Brocklehurst, called me Marion for most of the year.

At the end of grade seven, I went on to junior high. There were students from other elementary schools attending my junior high. It was an opportunity to introduce myself by a name that people could actually pronounce. "Hi, I'm MariaM," I said, using a flat "a" so my name rhymed with "MariaN." It was just easier and helped me to feel less alienated from what was already a difficult transition for me.

I was careful never to say my name this way at home, especially around my father. My father felt that I should be proud of my name, which meant saying it correctly. The

58

problem was, he had never been a teenage girl living in Victoria in the 1970s. I wanted to fit in, to be cool, to feel like I belonged.

One day, my father overheard me identify myself on the telephone using the "MariaN" pronunciation. He was angry. I knew he was right, but I justified my behaviour because the perception of my being considered as "different" began with my name. Throughout my teen years I continued to use the "MariaN" version outside of the house.

When I was twenty, I left Victoria to continue my studies at McGill in Montréal. In Montréal, people always got my name right. The fact that McGill had spelled my name properly on all my correspondence impressed me; this was already very different than my experience with the Victoria school system and the University of Victoria where I was constantly correcting my misspelled name.

I floated through my first few days at McGill. It was as though I had been transported to a fantasyland where everybody knew my name. I met students from all over the world – from India, the Middle East, and from countries in Africa that I had barely heard of. For the first time in my life, except when I was on family visits to Pakistan, everybody got my name right away.

"Mariam? Oh yeah, nice to meet you!"

"Mariam, hey my sister in Beirut has the same name as you!"

"Mariam? Oh, that's such an easy name. It's like Miriam but with an 'a'!"

I could hardly believe my ears! Almost overnight I stopped saying my name with the flat "a" and reverted to pronouncing it the way my father taught me. If people didn't get it the first time, then I patiently went over the pronunciation with them and was happy if they got a modified version with a soft, long "a" like "Maarium."

After my first term at McGill, I returned to Victoria for the Christmas holidays. Four months in Montréal and at McGill had already started to transform me from a shy girl who felt like an outsider into a more confident young woman who pronounced her name properly. Not too long after I arrived back in Victoria, I called one of my best friends on the telephone.

I said: "Hi, its Murr-yum."

There was silence on the other end of the line and then my friend said, "Who?"

"Hey Estelle! It's ME, Murr-yum. Murr-yum Pal. I'm home from McGill for the holidays."

"Oh, hi MariaM. I didn't recognize your voice."

Later, when we got together, I tried to explain to Estelle my newfound pride in pronouncing my name. I thought she would understand since she had a French name, but she looked at me blankly. She didn't really get it and I think she said something to the effect that it was my responsibility to adapt my name so the people in Victoria could pronounce it. This was to be the first of numerous differences between us, which arose after my move to Montréal. Our friendship disintegrated during the first summer that I was home from Montréal. I was enthralled by big-city life and found Victoria hopelessly pedestrian and boring. For Estelle it was home. That first summer we had a fight. Estelle said I had changed too much, and she didn't enjoy being with me anymore. In particular, she thought the way I said my name was stupid and affected. Many of my Victoria friendships suffered similar fates.

Eventually I decided to stay in Montréal and resolved to become bilingual. Mariam was easy to pronounce in French, although I did get called "Myriam" from time to time. A few years later, while working in Dakar, Senegal, my Senegalese colleagues started to call me "Mariama." I found it charming and for the first time in my life, I had a nickname.

My difficulties with my first name more or less disappeared over the next twenty-five years as I traveled widely, living in West Africa and Asia for ten years. Occasionally someone's spell-check would "correct" my name from Mariam to Miriam. Mildly irritating, yes, but it was manageable. In 2008, six years after returning to Montréal, I met Eli, who would become my husband. But my name problems returned when I met my future mother-in-law. Her name was Gertie. She and her husband Morrie were warm and gracious and welcomed me into their lives, inviting me for Passover dinner and playing Jewish geography, trying in vain to connect me to their world. I was finally able to understand what all those Woody Allen movies were about.

After a few stumbles, Morrie had my name down pat. Gertie tried and tried but somehow, she never was able to pronounce my name; she concocted a unique pronunciation that I had never heard before – Mary-HAMM. I was amused but also mildly irritated – I thought I had left all those name problems behind me.

Sensing my frustration, Eli tried his best.

"Listen to me carefully, Gertie – just say after me – Maariam. It's easy, eh?"

"Maaari-HAMM!"

"Gertie, no, you're not listening to me. I'll say it again. Maariam."

"Maari-HAMM!"

Eventually we just gave up. The rest of the family soon realized when she talked about "Mary-HAMM," Gertie was referring to me and it was just easier to go along with her. One day she spotted me from a distance in a mall and started shouting my name. Oblivious, I walked on, not tuning in to somebody screaming a name that didn't register. It was only when I returned home and heard her message on the answering machine that I realized that she had been calling me. The hilarity of it all was that despite hearing me say my name properly, all of Gertie's friends and some of Eli's older relatives mimicked her pronunciation. After Gertie died, Eli suggested that it would be a good idea if we taught some friends and relatives how to say my name correctly. One told us that she had noticed Eli and I said my name differently, but she assumed Gertie was right! I found this extraordinary – it has been my experience that everybody knows how to pronounce his or her own name. To this day, whenever I call Gertie's friends on the telephone, I make sure to identify myself as Eli's wife. If I say my name the response is, "Who is this, dear? Could you say that again?" Eli's wife is just easier.

Sarwar

My middle name is Sarwar. I was given this name to honour my paternal grandmother who bore this name. It is a Punjabi name, given to both boys and girls. Originally Persian, it means leader, chief, or lord. Like my first name, it's another tongue twister for native English speakers. This is because, like Arabic, Punjabi has consonants and no vowels. Thus, the proper pronunciation requires the tongue to roll from an "s" to an "r" sound and then quickly to a "wur" sound. While Mariam can at least look vaguely familiar – the eye sees what they think are the first two or three letters of a name like Miriam or Marion – this is not the case with my middle name.

While I acknowledge that my middle name has its challenges, I understand its significance and symbolism and appreciate why my parents gave me this middle name. Since I was a teenager, I have used the first letter of my middle name, "S," as part of my signature. This is my private homage to my grandmother and reminds me of how far the women in my family have come in three generations.

Sarwar Bhutt, my paternal grandmother, was married to her first cousin, my grandfather, when she was only a teenager. The arrangement had been planned since childhood. Sarwar never learned to read and write, and her education consisted of learning her prayers and reciting some Koranic passages from memory. Yet she married an educated man. Despite enduring the tragic deaths of her first five babies in infancy, Sarwar raised three sons to adulthood. After my father, who was the youngest, left

Pakistan, she waited for his letters, which my grandfather or one of my uncles would read to her.

I have very few memories of my grandmother. She died when I was eight years old, when it had already been five years since my last visit. But I have a photograph of us taken when I was three years old. She held me in her lap – I had a funny look on my face, almost on the verge of tears but she smiled at me with unconditional love.

I am ashamed to say that as a teenager I was embarrassed by my difficult middle name. I cringe, recalling that I said it stood for Susan, wanting to have at least one name that was easy to pronounce. I wanted a license plate with my name on the rack; I wanted to be like everybody else and to belong.

Pal

My mother used to tell a story about an encounter she had shortly after she married my father. As was the case in 1957, she had changed her surname to her husband's although she kept her maiden name as a second middle name. According to the story, asked for her name she replied, "Mrs. Pal." The person serving her replied, clearly waiting for the rest of the name, "Yes? Is that all?" My mother, somewhat taken aback, told him, "Yes, that is all, thank you." To which the gentleman replied, "Are you sure?"

I wish I had an equally delicious anecdote about my surname. Beyond the schoolyard taunts and predictable "you're my pal" remarks, my surname has been the object of curiosity over the years.

At New Delhi airport, the immigration officer examined my passport for what seemed an eternity. I began to feel nervous, wondering what the matter was. The officer looked up at me and said: "Good Madam, I am most curious. You have a Muslim first name, a Punjabi second name, and a Hindu Bengali surname. I must admit, Madam, I am puzzled." I smiled, breathed a silent sigh of relief, and told the officer a short history of the Pal name.

The surname "Pal" has its roots in Central Asia and, before that, in Hungary. My Middle Uncle explained the history of my father's family to me one day when I was visiting Lahore. The Pals were courtiers of Raja (Prince) Jah Pal, a Kashmiri Hindu prince. Three or four hundred years ago, two waves of Pals migrated from the mountains of Kashmir to the plains of Punjab where they converted to Islam. The other Pals moved further east to Bengal, remaining Hindus. My great-great-grandfather was a master weaver who made fine cashmere shawls and my great-grandfather was a trader. His sons pursued higher education with considerable success. *Dada Abajee* and his brother were able to complete their law degrees despite the fact that their father died suddenly when his sons were young. Their elder brother, winner of the All-India Gold Medals in both Mathematics and Arabic, left school and worked as a bureaucrat in the Punjab Canal Administration office to support the family.

The Pal name has unexpectedly drawn me into memorable conversations with two Nobel laureates. The first was in Dhaka, Bangladesh, in 1994, where I was part of an international group who took a training course at the Grameen Bank. The Grameen Bank is a Bangladesh-based

NGO that combats female poverty through micro-finance. Dr. Yunus, the bank's founder, ended up seated beside me at lunch. I introduced myself.

Dr. Yunus leaned forward, cocking an ear. "Excuse me, did you say your name is Mariam Pal? Pal?"

"Yes, that's right," I replied.

"But 'Pal' is a Bengali name – you don't look Bengali!"

To the consternation of the other guests, Dr. Yunus and I engaged in an intense discussion for the rest of the luncheon as our conversation meandered from the Pal family history to my parents and finally, my life and career. Dr. Yunus studied in the USA and married an American whom he later divorced. They had a daughter who hated Bangladesh and who did not know very much about her father's Bengali culture. Dr. Yunus asked me about my childhood, and we spoke of living between two cultures. When he won the Nobel Prize in 2006, I immediately thought of our interesting and wide-ranging talk twelve years earlier. I wondered what happened to his daughter.

About five years after I met Dr. Yunus, I attended a reception honoring the Nobel laureate economist Amartya Sen, also of Bengali origin. The hostess of the party introduced us.

"Your name is Pal? That's a Bengali name! You don't look Bengali!

"Are you married to a Bengali? You seem American to me."

"No, Dr. Sen, I'm a Canadian but my father is Pakistani – his name is Pal. We're Kashmiri, originally from Amritsar but the family migrated to Lahore in 1947."

"Extraordinary! But why is your name Bengali?"

"Dr. Sen, shall we sit down?" I said as I launched into my family history.

Mariam Sarwar Pal

My professional life is bilingual. Francophones have no problem spelling or pronouncing my name. Yet for decades I have had the same conversation, in French, with many francophone Québecois after I tell them my name.

"You're not from here are you?"

I answered, "Why do you say that? Is it my accent?"

"Oh no! You have a charming accent – like an American who learned French in France. Très cute! Well, your name – it's not from here."

Smiling, I responded: "Actually I was born in the Royal Victoria Hospital in Montréal. And my mother was from Northern Ontario."

"Really, how interesting. But tell me, what kind of name is 'Pal'? You're not really from here are you?"

I didn't miss a beat; "Well, it's a Canadian name now. But it has its origins in Pakistan. Kind of like how 'Tremblay' or 'Dion' are originally from France. You know what I mean?" At this point I smile sweetly. I have invoked this argument countless times. It usually brings the conversation to an end.

My parents chose my name with care; they wanted it to reflect who I was, yet not be too unusual or difficult. Growing up in Victoria, my name branded me as an outsider. I ached to buy my miniature license plates off the revolving rack. I wanted to be predictable, like cottage or cheddar. But then I discovered les fromages de Montréal, which led me to a rich world of fragrant cheeses and bold names. Like Mariam Sarwar Pal.

6

Pakistan and Me

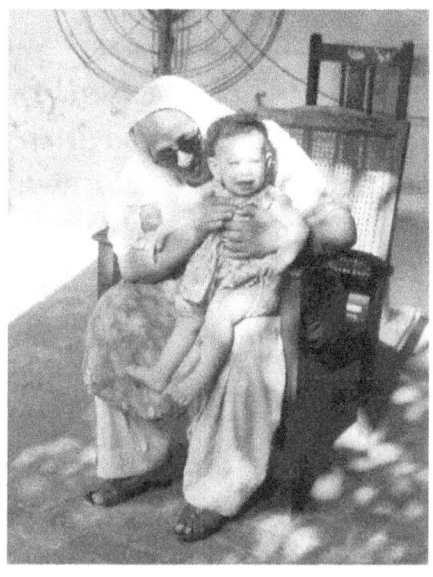

With my grandmother in Lahore, 1961

"Oh, my God, yes, I'll tell him right now!" Mrs. Maclean slammed down the phone and sprinted to the lecture room where a class was in progress. She opened the door and gestured wildly at the man teaching the class. "Professor Pal, your wife went into labour – she's at the hospital!"

The young professor froze for a second then regained his composure. "All right, class is dismissed for today. We will meet Friday at our usual time." Then he gathered his lecture notes and charged out of the classroom. It was a sunny,

September, Montréal afternoon in 1958. I was born as the late summer sun faded into evening.

My parents chose my first name with care, rejecting spectacular options like "Zaibunnissa," or "Khadija." They wanted my name to reflect the Pakistani Muslim heritage of my father but to blend into the Canadian world of my mother, Catherine. My father, Izzud-Din, wished that his father had chosen an easier name for him; even Pakistanis found it difficult. He wanted to be sure that his daughter would not be burdened with something too exotic. They decided that "Mariam," which means Mary in Arabic, was a good name for their cross-cultural baby. My name would be spelled with an "i" rather than with a "y" to discourage the temptation Canadians might have to call me "Mary" for short. But for my middle name, which is Sarwar, my parents honoured my Pakistani grandmother. Unfortunately, it is a name that is almost impossible for most of the world to pronounce properly – unless one speaks Urdu or Punjabi.

When I was a few weeks old, my father registered my birth with the High Commission of Pakistan in Ottawa. I was born Canadian, but he wanted to make sure that I had the option of Pakistani citizenship should both governments allow this in the future. Thus, as a baby my cross-cultural identity was established. I still have this document to which a photograph of me, three months old, is affixed. Baby me stares at the camera, transfixed and unseeing.

Lahore, 1959

As an infant of eight months and a toddler of nearly three years, my parents took me on two long trips to Pakistan in 1959 and 1961. These trips were also my mother's introduction to her new husband's homeland.

When I was older, I went to Pakistan with my father three times: in 1968, 1977, and 1980. The purpose of these trips was to reinforce the Pakistani identity that Papa thought I should have. These journeys were short: in total adding up to a mere five weeks of my life. Yet those thirty-five days were instrumental in establishing my identity not as a Pakistani, but as a Canadian.

Travels with my parents, 1961.

1959 and 1961: First steps in Lahore

McGill University, Montréal
Press release for June 8, 1959

Professor I. -D. Pal of McGill University Montréal is arriving in Lahore this week; he was recently awarded the Canada Council travel grant for advanced research. Prof. Pal has been on the staff of McGill University since 1955. Prior to that he was a member of the economic staff at the University of the Punjab, Lahore. Prof. Pal teaches international trade and econometrics at McGill University and is actively engaged in research on commercial policy and economic development.

At eight months old, I went to Pakistan via London, Oslo, Rome, and Cairo. A second trip followed in 1961. There would be other visits throughout the 1960s and '70s. While other Canadian families vacationed in Europe, Hawaii, or Disneyland, our family visited Pakistan.

Letters I discovered after my father's death confirmed that my father had desperately wanted to return to his country after completing his PhD at McGill. Insulted when Punjab University offered him his pre-PhD position at the same salary, Papa chose to live in Canada, a country where he had been welcomed so generously.

Reading Papa's letters, I understood for the first time just how deeply he felt the rejection by his own country. Did the conflict that my father felt throughout his life in Canada have its roots in the choice that he was forced to make between two countries? Like many first-generation immigrants, he was never completely at ease in either his adopted or his home country.

My mother, who had grown up Polish Catholic in Northern Ontario, ending up in Montréal via London, England, and Toronto, always spoke of Pakistan with affection. In 1961, after two trips to the country she thought she could live there.

"Life seems less artificial and less hurried. There is no television and barely any radio. I am feeling in quite Victorian times." [sic] Five years earlier, writing to a friend to tell her that she had married my father, she did not even mention the vast cultural and religious differences between herself and her new Pakistani husband. She sounds happy; she mentions how she and her new husband are so much alike.

My father's family was well-to-do by Pakistani standards and lived in a large house with many servants cooking, cleaning, and running errands. Meals appeared on the table, dirty clothing was returned, washed and ironed.

In 1959, I developed stomach problems almost immediately upon arrival. After a few days living in the family house, my mother visited the kitchen where she discovered, to her horror, that the cutlery and dishes were washed with cold water and ashes.

Following a serious discussion about sterilization techniques and bacteria with my grandfather, *Dada Abajee*, the head of the household, my mother convinced him that the kitchen was the source of my maladies. He ordered the kitchen staff to wash my dishes with soap and hot water. My health improved slightly but I remained weak and by the end of the four-month visit was on a liquid diet.

Summers in Lahore are legendary for their extreme heat; temperatures climb as high as forty-five degrees Celsius. In letters written to her best friend in Canada, my mother told of the languid days she spent supine, one hand turning the pages of her book, the other hand pulling the string of the old-fashioned hand-cranked ceiling fan.

Despite my poor health, it was in Lahore that I took my first steps. And it was in Canada where my mother bought my first pair of shoes at a children's shoe store on Queen Mary Road in Montréal. Fifty years later I married the son of the owner of that shoe store.

1968 – Two Weeks

Mr. Patrick folded the note from my mother, put it back in the envelope and said, "So are you looking forward to your trip?"

"Oh yes, Mr. Patrick, I can't wait to go to Pakistan. I haven't been since I was a baby – I don't remember anything. I have lots of cousins to meet and my grandfather, too. And it will be my first time on an airplane!"

I travelled to Pakistan with my father in December 1968. I was ten. My younger sister, Salma, had been born in 1963. Wary of her health, my parents did not want to take her to Pakistan until she was ten years old. So off I went to Pakistan with Papa while my mother and younger sister stayed home.

As the Pakistan International Airlines jet taxied down the runway at Orly, I suddenly realized that I had left my brand-new mod mustard suede handbag on the hook of the bathroom door in the Paris airport. My mother had purchased the handbag for me at Eaton's especially for the trip. She had warned me not to lose it. And I had! I broke down in tears. Prior to leaving Canada I had carefully put a comb, some tissues, and my December allowance inside. My father tried to console me, as did a kind stewardess who explained that was not possible for the pilot to return to the gate. She gave me a toy and some fashion magazines to cheer me up.

Shalimar Gardens, Lahore, 1968.

The whole family greeted us at Lahore Airport and garlands of marigolds were looped around my neck. When we got to my grandfather's house my father was so busy talking to his father and brother that he didn't notice that I gulped two Fantas, something my mother would never have allowed.

I quickly became the centre of attention. There were cousins to meet and play with and my grandfather to talk to. My relatives bought me balloons, laughed at whatever I said, and found everything about me absolutely fascinating.

Family and friends came to visit, bearing gifts and cake. Our visit coincided with *Eid* and a new red satin outfit was made for me.

I was used to my father's Pakistani food but what I ate in Lahore was either too spicy or tasted "funny." Within three days I was sick. As the visit wore on, I noted in my diary, "there is never anything good for breakfast."

I went everywhere with Papa: to buy gifts to take home, to his favourite bookstores, to visit some historical sites, and I even had my portrait taken by a friend of his who was a photographer.

My *Dada Abajee's* house was not like houses in Canada. There was no hallway and so to go from one room to the other I had to pass through an adjacent room. I found this very strange. The kitchen didn't look like anything I'd seen before. No cupboards, no counter or cookie jar full of oatmeal biscuits. But the worst was the ugly bathroom with no hot running water. I had to squat to use the toilet and pull a chain to flush it.

The milk, the toast, the eggs all tasted different from what I was used to. All I liked to eat were pastries. Luckily, there was a daily steady stream of cake brought by all the visitors coming to see my father.

I enjoyed having four cousins to play with – at home I only had one sister. But sometimes I felt as if they ganged up on me. One day, despite my protests, the cousins insisted on squeezing a dozen glass bangles onto my arm. Later that night I lay in bed and broke them off my arm, one by one, leaving a pile of broken glass under the bed. The bangles were so tight; there was no other way to remove them.

Despite my father's best efforts to rein me in, two weeks in Lahore turned me into a spoiled brat. A sugary diet, going to bed at all hours, and being the centre of attention were to blame. At age ten, Pakistan represented incredible freedom. It was like my birthday every day!

Life in Canada seemed dull and disciplined after two freewheeling weeks in Lahore. A few days after my return, I came home late from school. I had been given a detention for the first and only time in my life. Later, I heard my mother telling my father that she was glad I had been given a detention because I needed to "calm down." A detention sobered me up, but for many months I longed to be back in Lahore where I could eat cake and go to bed whenever I wanted.

In Murree, Pakistan, 1977

1977 – Two weeks

"But I don't want to go to stupid Pakistan! I'm eighteen years old; I need a summer job after my first year of university. I have to get contact lenses and some decent clothes."

My father was not impressed. "Mariam, it is nearly ten years since your last visit. You need to stay connected to your roots. I'll book us flights and we can leave after your final exams. And no, I will not pay for contact lenses for you."

"What's wrong with contact lenses? If you had your way I'd be wearing big ugly aviator glasses, my hair in a greasy braid down my back, some dumpy oversize shirt and pants and sensible shoes and I would never go anywhere or have any friends." But even as I spoke, I knew I had lost this battle. I was off to Pakistan.

Gently, my mother tried to make me see the positive side. "They are your family, and they are anxious to see you. Everybody is so warm there. It's important that you know where your father is from. And the shopping is great!"

I listened, skeptical. Ever since starting high school I had been at loggerheads with my father over almost everything. From placing limits on dating and on my attendance at high school dances, to using the car, to my 1 a.m. curfew, I felt that my father was impossibly strict. I was a good student but in all other aspects of my teenage life there was constant tension. During my first year of university, I found myself a red-haired boyfriend, failed calculus, and got a D in economics. It was a full-on rebellion.

We went to Pakistan in May, the hottest month of the year. The country was in the throes of a political crisis. Speculation was rife that a military *coup d'état* was imminent.

My father and I flew to Karachi from Athens. We were the only people to disembark in Karachi. I walked out of the refrigerated Swissair 747, down the airplane stairs and straight into a wall of humidity, laced with the pungent scent of rotting garbage and jet fuel. After a day in Karachi, we flew to Lahore.

Lahore was under a curfew that was only lifted from 5 a.m. to 7 a.m. daily so that people could buy food and other necessities. My father, who hates the heat, insisted that we stay at the Hilton because there were no air conditioners at my family's house. Even if there had been, frequent power cuts would have rendered them useless. Middle Uncle, a high-ranking bureaucrat, made sure we were issued curfew passes, allowing us to travel freely throughout the city.

Lahore assaulted me. The dry heat, in the low forties, was intense and debilitating. The neighbourhood surrounding the family home was now much more commercial than residential. The air was thick and hazy brown, the smells putrid, and the noise incessant. I noticed that there were chicken coops on the roof next door. Within a day of arriving, I was sick.

In the ten years since my last visit, much had changed. My grandfather had died. My father and Big Uncle had fought bitterly over the inheritance; they were no longer speaking to each other. The cousins I played with as a child were never spoken of and instead, I visited with other cousins who, along with Middle Uncle, now lived in my grandfather's old house. I wondered how I could have enjoyed myself so much ten years earlier. Where did all those wonderful memories come from? I felt overwhelmed but also bored; everything on the TV and radio was in Urdu and I had not thought to bring more books with me.

My family in Lahore told me I was home, that I was a Pakistani girl because my father is a Pakistani. But I felt Canadian. And confused. My spoken Urdu was poor and my Punjabi virtually nonexistent, so I was unable to communicate with most of my family except for Middle Uncle and one of my female cousins. Everybody else just shouted at me – as if hearing the words louder would make me understand.

Then there were my clothes. My father patiently explained to me that I needed to dress more modestly. We compromised; I wore long shirts or cotton dresses and loose pants. Despite being covered from head to toe, men stared boldly at me wherever I went. It was upsetting and humiliating. Walking into the hotel lobby with my father, groups of men having tea would stop talking to each other and stare at me as I approached, then stop and stare as I passed by. I could feel their eyes burning into my back as I walked into the elevator. It was like being an animal at the zoo. My father saw how mortified I was; he advised me just to ignore them. I found this impossible.

I told my cousin and other young women I met just how uncomfortable the staring men made me. They were sympathetic. However, they did not agree with me that the solution was to promote more respect for women in

Pakistani society. Rather, they told me that they just went out in public as little as possible. I was aghast.

مریم

"Salaam, Mariam, welcome! Please come here with me and we will join the ladies," said the young woman whose father we had come to visit. Before I knew what was happening, my father was whisked into a room to talk and drink scotch with the men, and I was herded into a room full of women. I could feel their eyes on me, curious, taking in my short hair, glasses, gold hoop earrings, and strange clothes. As always, tea was served.

"Mariam, my older brother is looking for a wife," said a young girl named Aisha, "are you interested?" The room erupted with high-pitched, girlish laughter.

"I don't know – I don't think so," I stammered. I wasn't prepared for this kind of question.

"I've only just finished my first year of university. I haven't decided what to do with my life. In Canada, most girls don't get married until they're in their twenties. I want to have a career and live in my own apartment."

"Live in your own apartment?" said one of the women. "Who will cook for you? You'll be so lonely! Sounds awful!"

"Yes, of course," said another woman, "you live in Ca-na-da, you are not used to our eastern ways."

Thankfully, the conversation shifted to a discussion of a wedding they had all attended recently. Their banter baffled me; I was used to talking about boys, music, movies, television, why my parents drive me crazy.

Trying to please my father, I exchanged addresses with some of the girls and after I returned to Canada we corresponded. But the letters stopped as the girls married young men chosen by their parents.

Two decades later, in a pub in London, my father and I were talking about the 1977 trip. Then Papa dropped a bombshell. One of his motivations for taking me on this trip had been to scout out possible husbands for me. But my mother had objected so strongly that he backed off. I remained calm, sipping my drink, as my father confessed. Later, nursing a drink on the plane from London, the enormity of how different my life would have been hits me. How could I have survived? What would have become of me?

مریم

My father's friends had come to talk politics. I sat beside him. The old brown ceiling fans whirled at top speed and even though I slumped directly below one of them, there was little relief from the searing heat. Hot air churned above me as I sipped my tea and tried not to wilt.

I was in my late teens, almost an adult in Canadian terms, but in Pakistan I remained a child. My status was that of a daughter. The only other possibility was as a wife. There was nothing else. The landing card in Pakistan, filled out upon arrival, asked females for the name of their father or the name of their husband. It doesn't matter whether the father is dead or alive, what is important is the connection to a male.

A couple of my father's friends spoke to me. The others studiously ignored me, politely addressing my father as they ask him, "What is she studying?" or, "How old is she?" or, "Does she speak Punjabi?" Knowing that in Pakistan it was considered polite not to address an unrelated woman directly, I still found it mortifying to listen to my father and his friends discuss me as I sat there silent, sweating, and isolated. I remained quiet and demure. It was still better than being with the women.

Returning to Pakistan as a young woman stunned me. I was totally unprepared for the restrictions that Pakistani society imposed on me. In Canada I had gradually gained more freedom and responsibility as I got older. When I visited Pakistan as a ten-year-old I enjoyed unfettered freedom and cake *à volonté*. At nineteen, I couldn't dress how I wanted to, was constantly gawked at by men and was plunged into a society where men and women are highly segregated. The oppressive heat, a political crisis, and unrelenting noise and air pollution further contributed to my alienation. My family and my father's friends kept on telling me that I was a Pakistani, but I had never felt so far away from home in my life.

1980 – One week

August 7, 1980 – Excerpt from my diary.

And now, India and Pakistan. Plunged again into the depths of a man's world. Two weeks of being stared at, treated like, in my opinion, a second-class citizen. It's my heritage, but aspects of it make me so angry. To treat women as second-class citizens – to cover them up, keep them at home makes me so mad I could scream. I have to learn tolerance, much more tolerance about these things.

August 16, 1980 – Excerpt from my diary.

I seem to have a love-hate relationship with this part of the world. Definitely I can only stand it in small doses. The gaps are tremendous between my world and this world and they are such as to make the latter seem threatening if I come too close in contact with it. The teeming populations, the seemingly endless stream of humanity, the poverty, the filth, the squalor, and the different cultures and languages surround me until they begin to build up like a wall that I can't seem to find a door or even an empty chink to peer through. As a woman, as a feminist, modern Western woman, I find it especially difficult. And having spent all of my life trying to figure out where I stand in between these two cultures, I finally decided that I am a North American woman now, first and foremost. This makes it very difficult for me to be broader, to cross cultures, for I feel that I have done, or have been forced to do this all my life. I don't know, I guess I find it all very confusing and bewildering still. Why was all this thrust on me anyway?

In the autumn of 1980, I would be continuing my studies at McGill in Montréal. Papa said he would like me to go with him to Pakistan a month before I was scheduled to leave Victoria. Initially I was not very enthusiastic about this trip, and then Papa made me an offer I could not refuse. He was going to Shanghai on business and then on to Pakistan via India. We could visit the Taj Mahal. I agreed.

84

I was twenty-two, three years older than on my last trip, more mature and thoughtful. I had clear goals and knew what adjustments and compromises were needed on a trip to Pakistan. I knew what to expect and I came prepared. Photographs show me wearing elegant cotton tops and pants that bowed to the requirement of modesty as well as to fashion. By now fitted with contact lenses, I wore huge dark glasses whenever I was out in public to guard against staring men. I would peer over my glasses and stare hard at men who were particularly aggressive. I enjoyed it when they turned away, embarrassed.

I was proud of how I managed to adapt and felt far more comfortable than I had three years earlier. Instead of spending time meeting giggling girls prattling about marriage, I contacted one of Pakistan's leading feminists and had tea with her. Whenever I accompanied Papa visiting friends, he made sure that I stayed with him. The ambivalence of 1977 had faded, and I felt like a Canadian visiting family in Pakistan.

Within hours of my arrival in Lahore I was sick. The weather added to my discomfort. August is the monsoon season when the humidity is high, and it can rain for days. My cousins insisted on dragging me to the *bazaar* to buy some fabric, stopping by a pharmacy to pick up some pills that they were assured would cure me. As the day wore on, I got worse, and my uncle decided that I should be taken to a local clinic in case I had malaria. Stepping into the waiting room I was assailed by the strong smell of stale urine. I promptly threw up in the clinic waiting room and was immediately taken to see a doctor who diagnosed influenza.

I was in bed for the next three days. This whittled down my visit to just four days. Compared to my previous trip, the political situation was relatively stable, there having been a coup d'état by the Army in July 1977. There was no curfew this time.

1984 – Many more weeks in Pakistan
Excerpt from my diary, May 1984.

I am aboard a flight to Islamabad and the old ambivalence has reared its head. I always feel so strange whenever I am on my way to Pakistan. I feel as though a part of me belongs there yet at the same time, as I get closer, I feel more and more like a foreigner. I am a stranger in a strange land, half and half. There are several mixed couples aboard the plane. Very young (my age) – I wish that I could tell them what they're in for. It's a lovely idea – mixing cultures, learning from each, yet in reality the story is quite different!

I returned to Pakistan four years later as a graduate student. The Canadian government hired me as a team member for an agricultural sector study for Pakistan. My job was to analyze the needs of rural women. I didn't know it, but my trip was to be the first of dozens that I would make to the country over the next twenty years. This trip was also the last one where I was incapacitated by illness. Could it be that once my mind felt at home in Pakistan, the rest of my body followed?

مریم

In the late 1990s I was working in Pakistan. Papa happened to be there also and arranged to stay in the same hotel as me in Karachi. We decided to take a cab to one of my favourite stores to get a present for my sister. I watched my father hail a cab in front of the hotel. I didn't say a word when he simply hopped into the back of the taxicab and told the driver our destination. Arriving at the shop, the taxi driver and my father became embroiled in a short but heated discussion about the price. It ended with my father slamming the taxi door.

"That goddamn taxi driver – just because we hailed a cab from the hotel, he wants a bloody fortune!" He shook his head. "How disgusting."

"It's not such a good idea to get into a taxi without negotiating the fare in advance," I said gently.

My father looked at me and laughed. "You're right, it's been too long, I completely forgot. You may have been born in the Royal Victoria Hospital, but you know Pakistan."

7

Muslim Breakfast

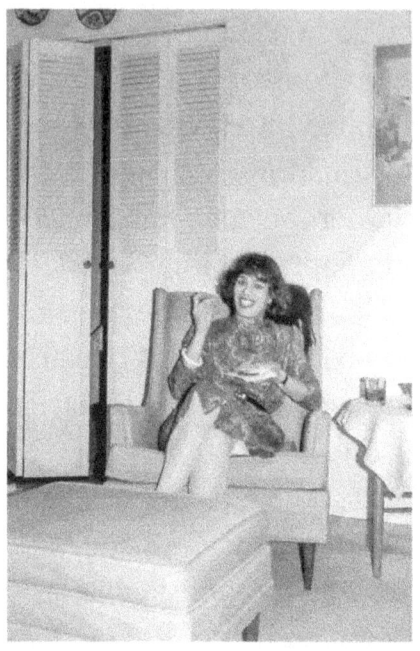

Mariam, 1985

"How disgusting!" said Papa, in a voice loud enough to be heard by our fellow diners who turned to look. A waiter holding aloft a steaming plate with a distinctive smell was passing by our table. Lowering his nose, Papa scowled and shook his head, then had a long sip of his martini.

"Papa, can you just quit it! You're embarrassing meee." I slid further down into the restaurant's banquette seat. I could feel the flush on my face. Please, please stop! I prayed silently. Why couldn't we just order our food and eat in peace? Did the whole restaurant need to know that we were

Muslims who didn't eat pork? It was bad enough that Papa interrogated the hapless waiter about almost every item on the menu and whether or not it contained pork. In 1970s Canada, there was little sensitivity to religious taboos on food.

I had not recognized the smell of sizzling bacon on the plate that sped past our table. At the time, it didn't occur to me to wonder how my father did. Many years later, when I met some of Papa's university friends, I figured out why. Back then, they told me with a chuckle, his favourite meal was bacon and eggs. When I confronted Papa with my newly acquired knowledge, he flatly denied ever eating bacon. His friends had made it all up. "Bunch of fibbers," he said, refusing to engage in the discussion any further. His denial was so vehement that I suspected his friends were correct.

I was raised in a relatively secular home. Yet from a young age, it was drilled into me never to eat pork. Ever. Papa taught me that while there was some flexibility (at least in my father's interpretation of Islam) regarding alcohol, no compromise was possible when it came to pork. My childhood was free of bacon and eggs, ham sandwiches, and pork chops. I don't recall it being a very big deal. After all, you don't miss what you don't know.

Islam stipulates that Muslims should not consume either alcohol or pork and requires that all meat eaten be *halal* (equivalent to kosher, animals are slaughtered following a proscribed ritual). When Papa came to Canada in 1955, *halal* meat was virtually impossible to obtain. Becoming vegetarian or giving up martinis were not serious options.

So, by the process of elimination, Papa adopted the pork prohibition rule. He applied it with evangelical zeal.

Papa had a keen wit, but he also had an irritating tendency towards using the same expressions over and over. One of them was referring to pork as "porcupine." He thought this was hilarious. Papa would regularly interrogate me to find out if, while dining out, travelling, or visiting friends, I had succumbed to the temptation of "porcupine." This continued well into my fifties. One evening, he came to dinner at my apartment. As he entered, he told me he smelled bacon.

"Yes, it's turkey bacon, Papa. I used it in some soup I made for my lunch. It's from an Iranian grocery store and it's *halal*. You want to see the package?"

"It doesn't matter. You're not supposed to eat bacon."

"Did you hear me, I said it's okay, it's fake bacon and it's *halal*."

Papa looked at me with disdain, sniffed, and said, "Porcupine. Disgusting. You're forgetting your roots."

"Since when have you turned into the religious police, Papa? Come on, let me make you a drink."

Papa liked to tell the story of the Air Canada flight that he took in the early 1970s where both choices of meal on his flight between Ottawa and Vancouver were pork, leaving him reduced to eating bread rolls, salad, and dessert. He made sure that everyone who heard the story understood that he made it a virtue to be hungry rather than eat pork.

My own encounters with the world of pork began after I moved to Montréal to study at McGill. My father did not want me to have a roommate because he was afraid that I would share a kitchen with a Christian pork-eater who would, after force-feeding me bacon and eggs, haul me off to church on Sundays.

"You're kidding," said Mandy, my Irish-Iraqi agnostic friend from statistics class. "You mean to tell me you never had bacon? Never?" Her father was a Kurdish symphony conductor.

"Nope. Never."

Several days later my buzzer rang on a Saturday morning. It was Mandy.

"I've got a present for you!" She held up a plastic bag and waltzed into my studio apartment. "Get out your frying pan – it's bacon and eggs for breakfast!"

As Mandy prepared the food, I told her what my father's friends had told me about his favourite meal in London and his denial.

"Mariam," she groaned. "He's such a douche bag. He got to do whatever he wanted but doesn't want you to have any fun."

My first bacon and eggs tasted delicious. It became a running joke between us. We called it "Muslim breakfast." But once the package of bacon Mandy had picked up at the local grocery store was finished, I couldn't quite bring myself to go to the store and buy a second package. Something stopped me.

At least now I knew the smell and taste of bacon. It was good and I could see why people liked it. But I had no idea what ham or roast pork tasted like. Breaking a lifelong taboo is a milestone. What's next? Should I mark this landmark with pride by eating bacon and eggs once a year just to prove to the world that I can? Should I incorporate these new foods into my diet? Was this even necessary? I had tried the forbidden pork.

At the supermarket, I studied the packages of bacon. I didn't feel very rebellious. Did I really want to buy bacon? The deliberate act of purchasing bacon or pork seemed so bold and brazen.

Not long after the bacon and eggs breakfast I started dating a Palestinian guy, Marwan. He lived with his brother. They were Christian. One evening, I stayed for dinner.

"This veal is delicious!" I said, looking up from my plate. As the words left my mouth and hung over the table, I caught the split-second glance that whirled around the table between Marwan, his brother, and his girlfriend. In that instant I knew that it wasn't veal I was eating but it was pork. They never said a word to me. But I knew.

Muslims and Jews share the pork taboo but in the Victoria I grew up in, Jews were about as scarce as Muslims. I never had a chance to trade pork stories with anybody. At McGill, I finally met some Jews. Many, like my friend Gary, had pretty liberal ideas when it came to pork. According to Gary, it was merely a question of semantics because "everybody knows that bacon and ham are not the same as pork!"

Decades later, I started dating a Jewish man, Eli, who was to become my husband. Early in our relationship, I was invited to a family dinner in a restaurant. I was astonished to see my future father-in-law order a bacon cheeseburger, and my future brother-in-law demolish a bacon pizza. Almost everybody at our table ordered a dish with pork in it except me. I was baffled. Thus began my education on complicated Jewish dietary laws and how they were complied with. Approaches varied. Some Jews openly consumed pork and bacon. Other Jews followed the rules at home but ate whatever they wanted when they were out. Some would never take home leftovers while others kept paper plates at home for the consumption of non-kosher food. The taboo, at least for Jews, was open to much more interpretation than it was for Muslims.

Eli had a good explanation. "You have to understand that the Jewish dietary laws are very strict and difficult to follow. So they bend them. Lots of Jews don't feel any less Jewish just because they have a bacon cheeseburger. They've integrated."

What Eli said made sense. I noticed the same type of behaviour amongst liberal Muslims. A hipster Egyptian Muslim encouraged me to try prosciutto for the first time.

"Mariam, it is divine. You will love this!" he said, putting a piece of melon and some prosciutto on my plate.

It was great, I had to admit. But would I buy some prosciutto to take home? Probably not.

I enjoy a little bacon from the breakfast buffet when I am on vacation. And I have been known to eat a *croque-monsieur* perched on a stool at the counter of my favourite restaurant, L'Express. But I have yet to try spareribs, pork roast, or a pork chop. I'm not really curious. I guess you could say that I like my pork in tiny doses.

8

Bicycles, birthdays, and Brownies

Mariam, 1963

The Chair looked at me and smiled. "We're almost finished. This is our last question." I nodded my head, smiled, and waited for him to start. I knew what they were about to ask. A list of possible questions had been provided to me prior to the interview and I was ready.

"Could you please tell us what, if any, experience you have in working with people who come from a different cultural or religious background than you?"

He looked a little embarrassed as he asked me this question, clearly meant for Canadians who did not come from a visible minority. The job at Canada's Immigration and Refugee Board I had applied for involved considerable interaction with immigrants. Exposure and sensitivity to different cultures and religions was therefore an asset.

I shifted forward in my chair and looked at the four people seated at the table. The air conditioning hissed in the background of the bland conference room in a downtown Montréal hotel. I took a deep breath, smiled, and replied.

"My background is unusual. Culturally, I am Canadian, but with the exception of my sister, I do not know of anybody else who has the same mixed roots as I do. My parents were a Polish-Canadian lapsed Catholic, and a secular Pakistani Muslim. Not surprisingly, our household had a unique culture. Throughout my life, I have constantly been a minority, challenged by the dominant societies in which I found myself: from growing up in Victoria, to living and working in Africa and Asia, and now as a resident of Montréal. So to answer your question, I have studied, worked, and socialized with people from cultures that are different from mine for all of my life. For me, this is normal."

My eyes scanned the interviewers. They looked at me; perhaps they did not know how to respond. "Thank you so much, Ms. Pal," said the Chair. We all laughed politely; we realized just how absurd the question was. Sitting there, what my parents used to refer to as the "turkey sandwich crisis" flashed into my mind. For a brief moment I considered sharing the story. I decided not to.

The interview was over. I stood up and shook the hands of each of the panel members.

"You must have had a very interesting childhood," said the only other woman to me, exiting the room.

"Yes, I suppose I did. But I didn't realize it. I just wanted to be like all the other kids."

She smiled. "Thank goodness you're not!"

Several months later, I was appointed.

مریم

I like to joke that I grew up in Canada's only Polish-Pakistani household. While I cannot provide definitive proof of this statement, I have yet to meet another person with my ethnic pedigree. Canadian restrictions on immigration from Pakistan meant that only a trickle of Pakistanis settled down in Canada during the 1950s and '60s.

Despite being raised on opposite sides of the world, my mother, a lapsed Catholic from Northern Ontario and my father, a Pakistani Muslim, had common core values. Together, they forged a distinctive family culture; cosmopolitan and highly literate, yet often oddly out of touch with the world just outside their front door. The Beatles, Halloween, and Thanksgiving were not on their radar. My parents were well-travelled, well-read, and well-rounded. They always knew what to do or say in an awkward situation or how to choose the right words for a condolence letter. I am forever grateful for everything I learned from them. But once I started school, it was hard to stem the tide of Canadian culture that flooded in. When I walked out the door every morning to go to school, it was as if I temporarily shut the door on my family culture, only to step back inside at the end of the day. My parents did a lot of things differrently. Others they didn't do at all. Thanksgiving, for example.

The turkey sandwich crisis was memorable. How could my parents have known that their indifference to Thanksgiving would result in their daughter being singled out because of what was between two pieces of bread in her pink lunchbox?

"I was the only one . . ." I stopped in between sobs to catch my breath, "the only one in my class who didn't have a turkey sandwich. I had my stupid peanut butter sandwich."

Mummy dabbed my eyes with the folded handkerchief she always kept inside the sleeve of her sweater. She handed me a glass of water and I gulped it down, warm tears rolling down my face.

"Yesterday was Thanksgiving. How come we didn't have a turkey?"

Mummy listened to me and gave me a big hug. "I'm so sorry, Mariam. Shall I make you some cocoa? Would it make you feel better?"

That evening, I overheard my parents talking in the living room. My mother told my father about the turkey sandwiches.

"We didn't celebrate Thanksgiving in Chapleau," said my mother, referring to the town in Northern Ontario where she had grown up.

"I always thought it was an Anglo-Saxon tradition, something that the Protestants do."

"Well, Victoria is certainly a bastion of Anglo-Saxon tradition, isn't it?" He continued,

"I like turkey. I guess we'd better make it next year for Thanksgiving." Then he laughed and my mother joined in.

And so, we had Thanksgiving turkey every year.

مریم

Throughout my teenage years, hunkered down in the trenches of adolescence, I felt like I was fighting one and a half cultural battles. On the eastern front, I fought Papa and his Pakistani girl ideal, while on the western front, in a half battle, I was up against small town Ontario Catholicism during the late 1930s.

From the time I turned twelve, my father and I were on a collision course. Our relationship reminded me of those bumper cars that used to be found at amusement parks. I was always roaring up behind Papa and bumping him. BOOM!

Papa thought that I should study hard in school and stay home the rest of the time except for occasional family outings. I think he fantasized that I would miraculously skip the teen years, get a degree, then meet and marry a perfect (in his eyes) man from Pakistan. I would have a long braid down my back and wear gold-rimmed aviator glasses. Instead, Canada served him up a red-blooded, genuine teenager. Papa was astonished with my obsession about how I looked and my passionate interest in makeup, clothing, and boys. When I had my waist-length hair cut in a shoulder-length bob at age sixteen, Papa was furious, snarling, "Girls should have long hair." His staunch opposition to contact lenses was because, "Girls shouldn't look pretty. Nobody will take you seriously if you look too pretty."

But I was determined. With each passing day, I wanted to be more Canadian than ever. I didn't like being different. I wanted to belong, to fit in. I wanted to do things: go to the dances, swim on Friday nights, cheer on my school rugby team, and more. Most of the time Papa said no and usually my being Pakistani was the reason. He would often justify his decision by comparing my childhood to his. I hated these analogies and used to call them sermons.

Pakistani culture, as interpreted and applied by my father, was based on denial. Denial meant that I couldn't go to sleepovers (bacon might be on the breakfast menu) or sing "Autumn Leaves" at City Hall with my class choir (according to Papa, choirs were for Christians only). I had wonderful childhood memories from my trip to Lahore as a ten-year-old. It had been non-stop play, cake, and Fanta. But maybe things had changed. Pakistan seemed to have become a bleak place where nobody had any fun.

By the time I was twelve, my blue bicycle was too small for me.

"Papa, please can you buy me a ten-speed bike? One with racer handlebars? It's what I really want."

"Absolutely not, Mariam," said Papa. "Why on earth do you need ten speeds on your piddly bicycle? You just ride from home to school and back. It's not as if you're competing in the *Tour de France*. You're going to get a regular bicycle from the Sears catalogue."

And then came the sermon.

"Mariam Pal, you have no idea of how lucky you are. When I was a young man, I was grateful to have my plain black bicycle. I used to ride in the blistering sun of Lahore and Amritsar several times a day going to my classes at college and later university. I never complained. I was glad to have it."

Another dumb story about perfect Papa, I thought. Even the bicycles were black.

"Geez, Papa, my life is totally different. Ten-speed bikes were probably not even invented back when you were a kid!"

Papa opened the catalogue to the bicycle section.

"Do you want the gold colour or the red?" I knew the subject was closed. A few days later the bicycle arrived (in gold) and my father assembled it. My new bike was so old-fashioned! I hated it and it sat in the garage, unused, week after week. Even though I loved getting home from school quickly on my bike, if my only choice was the new gold one, I preferred to walk. From time to time my father would look at it and mutter something about how spoiled I was and that nobody needed ten speeds on a bike!

The adjustment from elementary to high school had been tough for me. Nancy, my only friend from elementary school, was switching to private school.

I cast my eyes around the crowded cafeteria. Everybody had a friend to eat lunch with. Except me. This was the third day in a row that I was going to eat my lunch alone before heading to the library where I would listen to music or read.

"There now, it's always hard at the start of the school year, Mariam," said Mummy softly. "Here, take a tissue. There's so many new kids, I'm sure you will find a friend soon." Every afternoon after school, I sobbed at the kitchen table. Then my father had an idea. Why not come and have lunch with him in his office? It was not too far from school. I remember joining him a few times. Things did get better, and I don't remember having lunch by myself in grades nine and ten.

A year after my father bought me the gold bike, he and I were at Woodward's Department store in Victoria. It was June 1972, and I had just finished my first year of junior high.

"Papa, look at this bicycle. You say you don't want me to get a ten-speed bike because nobody needs so many speeds. How about a five speed? And it has the racer handles. It's not too expensive. Can I get it please? Please?"

The turquoise bicycle fit in the back trunk of my father's Dodge Dart sedan. I loved my bike and rode it for years.

مريم

Birthdays were our family's Christmas and Easter rolled into one. Birthdays meant a special dinner, the good china, and a homemade layer cake. Even now, I expect to do something special on my birthday – a consistent and uninterrupted tradition that goes back to my earliest childhood memories. Most other families viewed Christmas as the big event but at the Pals it was birthdays.

Papa thought that birthdays should be properly celebrated every year. He had not grown up with this tradition. He had not been sure of his real birthdate for the first three decades of his life. At the time that he was born in British India, mandatory birth registration did not exist. Like many immigrants to Canada, he did not have a birth certificate, but the government accepted an early Pakistani passport as proof of his date of birth. After he died, I found it amongst his papers. My father's official date of birth was January 22, 1926; it was used throughout his life. But his mother told him he had been born at the height of summer.

My mother raised the topic with her father-in-law on one of their trips to Lahore. Incredibly, my grandfather's tiny pocket-sized yearly agendas stretching back more than fifty years had somehow survived Partition. *Dada Abajee* studied his agendas for the 1920s. He found an entry made on June 22, 1925, that a third son had been born. They finally knew the precise date. My father wisely decided not to take on two countries' bureaucracies and chose not to correct the official records.

It had been *Dada Abajee* who changed Papa's birthday to January 1926. Concerned that his sons should have as many career options as possible, he modified his youngest son's birthday so that he could be eligible to write the Indian civil service exam twice. This exam, if passed, was the ticket to a stable life and a good career path.

On my birthday I was allowed to have my milk in a blue cocktail glass when I came home from school. The celebrant chose the birthday dinner menu. Papa's never varied: steak, potatoes, salad, and an orange cake for dessert. As for me, my favourite meal changed yearly. One year I chose a Pakistani dish for my birthday dinner – lamb and sour cream – an aromatic Kashmiri style dish perfumed with freshly ground cinnamon. Usually, Mummy baked the birthday cake at home, but the year I turned fifteen I convinced my mother to buy a cake. The bakery asked my mother what message to put on the cake. I chose a typical '70s expression, "Keep on truckin' – 15!" to commemorate my age. Mummy thought it was hilarious and talked about this for years afterwards.

مریم

"Brownies?" said Papa. He looked at my mother, puzzled. "Are you nuts? Why would I allow my daughter to participate in an activity with such a name?"

"All right, calm down and listen to me," said my mother. "Brownies are a club, like the Girl Guides. Mariam wants to join them. They have a branch at her school and girls are signing up."

"Well, you know I rely on you on such matters. What is this 'Brownies' business all about?"

"Mariam brought home some literature from school. I read it yesterday. Here – I'll show you."

"No, I don't want to read it. Tell me what it says."

Mummy gave Papa a long look over the top of her glasses. She opened up the brochure and pointed to the illustration.

"Look at this brochure – they talk about encouraging girls to grow up and be nurses and teachers. Not scientists or pilots. From what I can see, the girls earn badges for domestic activities. Hmm. Baking a cake, sweeping the floor. I don't think that Mariam should be encouraged to be part of this group. She can learn these things at home. Earning a badge for sweeping the floor – ridiculous! Oh, yes – there is also an expensive uniform to buy. She'll only wear it once a week for a year, maybe two. I think it's a waste of money."

Papa nodded his head in agreement.

Some girls in my class signed up and every Wednesday they wore their brownie uniform to school: shirt, skirt, socks, hat, and a special scarf around their neck. I loved the scarf. After school, before going to their meeting, the Brownies completed their outfits by putting on their sashes. All the sashes were crowded with badges and pins.

Tina Marie proudly pointed to one of her badges. "See. It's a baton-twirling badge. And this is for housekeeping, and I got a baking badge for baking cookies with my Mom."

The badges looked great. I thought about them while Mummy talked.

"Mariam, I know how much you want to be a Brownie," my mother said. "But there are other things you can do besides baton twirling or baking brownies. Why don't you join the book club that meets on Saturdays at the library downtown?"

I listened but didn't respond. How could I make Mummy understand that being a Brownie was like joining a special club, something very different from a book club at the library? I wanted to belong, to wear the uniform.

Decades later, it occurs to me that it was odd that I was not allowed to be a Brownie, supposedly because it encouraged little girls to be homemakers. Yet my mother ensured that I became very accomplished with what used to be called the "domestic arts." My friends jokingly call me the Canadian Martha Stewart because I cook, sew, bake, preserve, mend – you name it, I probably do it.

My parents may not have allowed me to be a Brownie, but they couldn't avoid the phenomenon known as "grad."

Like every other seventeen-year-old in town, I was eagerly anticipating my high school graduation. Preparations began months in advance. The big issue, apart from whether or not I would have a boyfriend to go to grad with, and of course how I would get alcohol, was the dress. In 1970s Victoria, only a handful of girls who came from well-to-do families got their dresses in Vancouver or even further afield. Most of us shopped locally or sewed our own dress.

My parents thought the whole grad experience was completely overdone. They could not understand my excitement. Several times a week Papa reminded me that "in Canada every Tom, Dick, and Harry graduates from high school. I don't see what the big deal is about." Mummy was more supportive. She thought that stretching grad into an entire weekend was "just a bit too much, don't you think?"

Given the attitude of my parents, it was not surprising that my request for a special allowance to buy a graduation gown was turned down. After some searching, I found a pale blue dress with a matching marabou-trimmed jacket on sale at Eaton's. Pale blue is not a good colour for me, and in hindsight the whole style was a little bit "mother of the bride," but I felt glamourous! I remember doing a special manicure of beige and pale blue. Unusually for me, I cannot remember what shoes I wore.

Papa refused to attend my high school graduation. I pleaded with him to come, but he was adamant. I remember fighting tears when he took a photo of me in my dress on our sundeck. He invoked various reasons to justify his behaviour.

"Oh, I attended too many ceremonies in my youth. I never attended any of my own graduations so why should I go to yours?"

I suspect that he didn't attend this and other ceremonies partially because he didn't understand the significance of such events in other people's lives because he never gave them a place in his own life. My mother attended my graduation ceremonies on her own.

Papa relied on my mother to steer him through Canadian teenage culture. After all, she had grown up in Canada, hadn't she? Neither one of them really took into account how much had changed in the three decades since Mummy's coming of age during the Depression and the war years. My mother had difficulty understanding my consumerism, and my interest in makeup and my appearance. She found it difficult to reconcile these teenage obsessions with my obvious ambition to be an architect or lawyer. I grew up in a time of great prosperity and increasing affluence; my expectations of life reflected this. As I stepped into adolescence, the pressure on my mother increased as I made more demands and asserted my independence.

"Mariam, you have so many clothes," she would say when I told her that I needed a new outfit for the next high school dance. But being Canadian, she understood that I wanted to go out, have friends, and have fun.

I somehow knew that something was different about our house. For years, I assumed that some of Papa's odd habits and rules were Pakistani. He always ate early, did not like unexpected visitors, and was very private. Once I got to know Pakistan, I finally understood that Papa was very different from most Pakistanis, who eat dinner late, love to go out, and welcome friends and relatives who drop by. What my father passed off as Pakistani was really just his own way of doing things. One thing which his family all agreed on was that he was "very difficult." I learned that Pakistani society was a much more open and social one than I could have ever imagined. The phone was always ringing, and visitors would appear at the door. My cousins went on school trips out of town, so why had I not been allowed to go on school trips in Canada?

When Papa left Pakistan, the country remained, in his mind, frozen in time. He had grown up in the '30s and early '40s, but several decades later Pakistan had evolved. The middle and upper classes all mimicked Western ideas and practices. School trips and talking on the telephone were two of them. My father had grown up in a household where there was no telephone, so he never really developed the habit of talking on the phone.

مریم

After graduating from law school, I was hired as an intern by a large firm in downtown Montréal. A special event had been organized – a seminar on working cross-culturally. The day after the seminar was announced, Janet, my boss, stopped by my desk.

"Oh, by the way Mariam, about that seminar on culture," she said. "You don't need to attend. From what I know of you and your background I bet you could teach it with your eyes closed." She smiled and I grinned back, thinking of the stories I could tell her. If she only knew.

9

Praying at the Altar of Food

Mariam, 1984

When I was growing up, dinnertime was sacrosanct. Children were expected to behave and to ask to be excused from the table. Our dining room was not just for special occasions and guests; we ate there nightly. The kitchen table was for breakfast and lunch, never dinner.

Good food was more than a way of life – it was a daily ritual not to be interrupted, least of all by the jarring ring of the telephone.

"Bloody uncivilized, calling at dinnertime. Lousy manners." My father, never one to mince words, growled away in the background.

"Laurie, I'll-call-you-back-after-dinner-okay?" I hissed into the receiver and sat back down at the table.

I gored my fish with my fork while Papa droned, "All civilized people know not to call between 5 and 7p.m... ."

My parents were passionate about food. We never went to church, nor did we worship Hockey Night in Canada. Instead, we prayed at the altar of food. In our house, food was plentiful, flavourful, and international. The world paraded through my parents' kitchen.

In addition to the standards such as *The Joy of Cooking*, a floor to ceiling bookshelf in a corner of the kitchen was crammed with cookbooks for cuisines from Indonesian to Italian. Tattered accordion files overflowed with newspaper clippings of recipes, pieces of cardboard with recipes cut out from boxes, and scribbles written on the back of envelopes. My parents subscribed to *Gourmet* magazine long before "foodie" and "food porn" were common parlance. Back then, food television meant watching a grainy, black-and-white Julia Child flipping an omelette with flair or showing us how to make *boeuf bourguignon*.

When my family traveled, we made pilgrimages to restaurants that had been reviewed in *Gourmet* magazine or written up in the *New York Times*. My father would save the clippings in battered brown envelopes rescued from the garbage. Each one bore a label of either a city and/or a continent. When we left for our trip, the envelope for that city or country was already packed in one of our suitcases.

My parents sought out the best food and drink available at our destination with the fervour of eighteenth-century missionaries. As a teenager, I often ordered meals in restaurants that I had read about in books. My memories of family restaurant meals range from lobster thermidor, Caesar salad made at the table, and the dramatic flair of cherries jubilee. Even now, I remember the exquisite taste of the melted ice cream and fruit.

I followed Alice Waters, Chez Panisse, and the growth of California cuisine from the beginning. Years after I purchased the first Alice Waters cookbook, I finally dined at her restaurant in Berkeley, California. We reserved a month in advance. When I gushed to the maître d' that I had been a fan for so many years he took me on a tour of the kitchen.

English tea and weekend curries

Growing up in the 1930s in what was then British India, my father never needed to cook. The family was well off and could afford full-time help. In 1950, at the age of twenty-five, Papa went to London for two years to attend graduate school. In England, he developed a lifelong fondness for pubs and English beer. But aside from the Guinness, British food was bad and bland. The *tsunami* of immigration from former colonies that would transform British food and make tandoori chicken a national dish was in the distant future.

Beyond the generic "curry," the English whom my father encountered in London had little or no knowledge of the breadth and sophistication of Indian or Pakistani cuisine. Papa loved to talk about the time a British friend brought him to a swish dinner party in London. The English hostess was surprised that my father wore a suit and tie, ate with a knife and fork, and politely turned down her offer to replace the Wedgewood plate with a banana leaf.

"She was expecting a half-naked Gandhi in a loincloth and sandals," Papa said. Today, even the smallest grocery store in England stocks Indian-style chutney, and "curry" is the foundation of what foodies refer to as British-Asian cuisine.

Until 1954, nine years after WWII ended, England rationed staple foods such as flour, sugar, eggs, and meat. Papa told me that he was only allowed one egg per week.

I was incredulous. "Did you say only one egg per week?"

"Yes, Mariam, but I also had an allowance for bacon which I traded easily for more eggs. A few months after I arrived," Papa explained, "I happened to learn of a fellow student who kept chickens. As he had graduated, he gave me some laying chickens which I kept in a small enclosure behind my flat." He smiled and laughed. "It was a classic barter system – basic economics. I had an excess supply of eggs, which I traded for extra portions of meat and sugar. A textbook case."

When he arrived, Papa ate at pubs or at one of hundreds of fish and chips shops that flourished throughout London. Nobody seems to know why, but this typical English meal, traditionally served in discarded newspapers, was not subject to wartime rationing. After a while, this narrow diet got tedious and expensive. Not only did Papa miss his own food but soon even cheap restaurant meals proved to be beyond his modest exchange-controlled budget.

"My funds were severely limited – not because my father could not afford to send me more money but rather due to the severe controls that were imposed by the Government of Pakistan on our purchase of foreign exchange such as British pounds. It was impossible for me to get a penny more than the amount sanctioned by the Pakistani government. The other Pakistani students I met suggested that I learn to cook."

Papa shrugged his shoulders. "The funny thing was that although I knew many people who were studying abroad, nobody mentioned anything to me about food when I inquired about student life in England. Nor did I even think to ask – I took food for granted. Had I known, I could have brought some spices, cooking pots, and other things with me. I could have learned to make a dish or two while I was still in Pakistan. When I left for London, I barely knew how to make tea!"

Papa decided to teach himself how to cook. He consulted books, quizzed fellow Indians and Pakistanis, and experimented. Gradually, he built up a basic repertoire of dishes and was able to feed himself on his small allowance. Like all novice cooks, he had some culinary disasters. A story that became part of our family lore was about how Papa, faced with an insufficient supply of butter, a rationed food, decided to use peanut butter to grease a pan. Each time he told the story, he laughed at his own ignorance. "I had to throw the pan out. It was completely burnt and the smell in my tiny flat was horrible!" he recollected, between howls of laughter.

Tea in a samovar or in a teapot?

My mother's food pedigree was Eastern European. Stanislas and Wilhelmina, my maternal grandparents, were ethnic Poles who came to Canada from the Ukraine just after the First World War. They met and married in Montréal but settled in Chapleau, Ontario, where my grandfather had a job throughout the Depression working for the Canadian Pacific Railway. I wish I knew more about my mother's family. She died when I was in my late twenties, well before I had an interest in her family history.

Growing up, my mother and her six younger siblings ate plenty of the cabbage, potatoes, beets, and dill, which my grandparents grew in their garden. Stored in the root cellar or transformed into sauerkraut, these hardy vegetables fed the family through long, harsh Northern Ontario winters. Mummy acquired her lifelong love of blueberries in her childhood when the entire family used to go on blueberry-picking excursions. She always said that her blueberry pies paled in comparison to her mother's. I never tasted my maternal grandmother's blueberry pie but my mother's was a delight – flaky crust full of fruit and sweetened just the right amount.

At seventeen, my mother quit school and moved to Toronto where she lived in a women's residence, Willard Hall, run by the Temperance Union. She loved to eat chocolate pie at her favourite Toronto restaurant, Basil's. The restaurant was still open in Toronto in the early 1970s when she took the whole family there for a slice of the famous chocolate pie. She was disappointed; the pie didn't taste as good as she remembered. I remember feeling underwhelmed by the whole experience. I was too young to understand the power of food nostalgia.

Mummy dreamt of a career in the theatre. Subsidized by her parents, she sailed across the Atlantic to try her luck in London. Sixty years later at the Immigration Museum in Halifax, Nova Scotia, I found her name on the passenger list for a ship traveling from Halifax to Southampton in 1950. She had indicated her occupation as "Artist"! Coincidentally, my parents both lived in London from 1950 to 1952 but their paths never crossed.

After two years in London, my mother was no closer to a theatrical career than when she arrived. Her parents could not afford to support her any longer, so she went back to Chapleau. It must have been agonizing to return to small-town Ontario after two years in beleaguered, but still cosmopolitan, London.

Her younger sister recalled with amusement that, unlike my father who learned to cook the food he had grown up with when he left home, my mother cast aside her Polish heritage, adopting British traditions, including food. There were fights and disagreements in the family home as my mother, fresh off the boat from London, insisted on making tea English-style instead of in a samovar in the Russian way of her parents. For the rest of her life, Mummy loved marmalade, chutney, sherry, and lemon curd. When we were children, she would bring bread and cheese for a picnic and called it a ploughman's lunch. I always thought that she had made this up until many years later when I was in London and saw it listed on pub menus.

Despite her proclivity towards all things English, my mother made sure that we appreciated Eastern European food. As a child, one of my favourite lunch dishes was cottage cheese mixed with a little bit of sour cream, sprinkled with dill, and served with pickled beets. Borscht and honey cake were also served up on a regular basis. Dishes that take hours to prepare like cabbage rolls and pierogies were a rare treat. From the time that I was in my early teens, my mother was a student, first at college and later at university. Mummy was more interested in spending her days at the library or at her desk reading Japanese history or practising her Russian vocabulary rather than in the kitchen preparing pierogies.

By the mid-1950s, my mother had landed in Montréal where she worked as a secretary and shared an apartment on Durocher Street with two of her siblings. "Kate did most of the cooking," said my aunt, Big B, calling my mother by the name her family always used. "Mostly meat-and-potatoes stuff, but she also introduced us to curries which she learned to make in London."

When my parents met in Montréal in 1956, my father was already an accomplished home chef. He returned to Pakistan for three years after completing his studies in London in 1952. To the great amusement of the entire household, he spent time in the kitchen observing and taking notes as the family cook and his mother chopped and sautéed, making daily meals.

"They all thought I was mad to live somewhere where I had to do my own cooking," Papa explained. "Nobody could understand it."

Taking a break from his PhD studies, Papa often cooked for his friends in Montréal on the weekend; this tradition continued after he married my mother. Big B remembers visiting my parents on Sundays when my mother was pregnant with me. The tiny apartment was full of the fragrant smells of ginger, garlic, and turmeric as my father, wearing his undershirt and shorts, quaffed beer, and cooked dinner for the three of them.

Poland meets Pakistan

When it came to food, my parents' cultures and temperaments rose above the challenges they faced in the other aspects of their lives and intersected almost seamlessly. Their marriage was based on a special recipe. Mix two strong personalities with a cup each of cultural and religious traditions. Add the following ingredients to taste: curiosity, new ingredients, and as many cuisines as possible. Add a smidgen of chance. Simmer for thirty years, take some risks, and serve with lots of love.

Both of my parents truly appreciated each other's cuisines, albeit with some reservations. My mother's stomach never tolerated hot chillies and my father was indifferent to the muffins and quick breads that were constantly coming out of the oven while we were children. For Papa, cake had to be sweet and moist. His annual birthday cake was a syrupy orange cake reminiscent of Pakistani desserts. Despite his initial reluctance, as the years progressed, my father grew to appreciate oatmeal cookies and the occasional piece of chocolate cake.

Mummy introduced my father to pickled beets, dill pickles, sauerkraut, and dark rye bread. He loved them all. Our fridge was always stocked with dill pickles. A few days before he died, knowing that I was coming over to visit, my father asked me to bring him some fresh pumpernickel and black Russian bread.

"And don't forget, Mariam, I don't want the bread sliced. I'm not an invalid."

After filling his order, I took a deep breath as I waited for the light to change, inhaling the scent of fresh bread. Whenever I go to this bakery and smell the pungent aroma of Eastern European breads, I always think of my father.

The clerk in the Eastern European delicatessen in downtown Montréal eyed my father's purchases: a jar of sauerkraut, some pickles, and a loaf of caraway seed bread. She scrutinized his brown face and snow-white hair, obviously puzzled: "But Sir . . ." she seemed to want to warn him that this was not his food. She had a worried look on her face. Did this man know what he was about to pay for?

Papa reassured her: "My dear late wife was Polish. I learned to love these foods from her. So don't worry, I know exactly what I'm buying." Still handsome in his eighties, Papa flashed her a dazzling smile and reached for his wallet.

As my father aged and his world became smaller, food was the best way to cheer him up. After he turned eighty-five, he was no longer able to drive, so I took him on food-focused expeditions around town. These outings would usually involve going to one of Montréal's cafés where he would order an espresso and a croissant. Our roles had reversed – when I was a child, he would be the one who would buy me an ice cream cone or a chocolate bar. Now I was looking for the handicapped parking spot, getting his walker out of the car, and making sure he had everything he needed. Papa cooked until the end. Admitted to hospital, gravely ill, the emergency room doctor was surprised that my father had cooked his own dinner the night before – fish.

Feeding family and friends

In the '60s and '70s the spicy food of the Indian subcontinent was mod and exciting. Invitations to my parents' dinner parties, featuring my father's Pakistani cooking, were sought-after.

Well, not always. My mother prepared beef stroganoff for a dinner. One of the invited couples exchanged furtive glances and barely touched their food. Mummy concluded that, apprehensive at the thought of being served spicy food, they had eaten at home before coming. Apparently beef stroganoff was not what they were expecting at our table.

My parents were generous with food and hospitality. They regularly held dinner parties. As children, and later as teenagers, we were expected to help prepare the food or set the table. We greeted the guests and conversed with them. I never wanted to go to bed when my parents were entertaining. I would lie on the floor of my bedroom, just inside the door, listening to the sounds that traveled down the hall to my room: the tinkling of the silver against the pink-and-blue "good" china, the laughter, and the faint strains of Dave Brubeck on the stereo.

One night I fell sound asleep, on the floor, in my pyjamas, my head framed by the door and the rest of my body splayed out into my bedroom. My mother came to check on me. Her laughter woke me up. Mortified at being discovered, I jumped up and dove under the covers.

Whenever there was a new professor or student of South Asian origin at the university, my parents would invite them home for dinner. Asian guests were impressed by my father's skills in the kitchen and grateful for an evening away from their hotel or temporary lodging.

Not all my parents' evenings were successful. Once they invited a dozen students from Pakistan, India, and Sri Lanka to our house. In Canada for specialized training, they were lodged at the university residences and fed a diet of institutional food. After some discussion at the morning tea table with my mother, Papa decided to roast a turkey. It was close to Christmas. The roasted bird was displayed at one end of the buffet table with my father carving. At the other end, side dishes and vegetarian options had been prepared to accommodate the various dietary restrictions of the group of students. To my parents' dismay, the Pakistani students wouldn't eat the turkey because it wasn't *halal*, i.e., slaughtered according to religious traditions. *Halal* is similar to kosher. I can't remember what my parents did or what those students ate but I know we had turkey for days . . .

Mummy refused to make what she called "boring Canadian food," such as beef stew and brownies. When one of her sisters and her husband came to visit from Ottawa, she knew just what to prepare for them. John, my mother's brother-in-law, liked plain food. My mother was happy to oblige.

"Why, I will make them a plain beef stew," announced Mummy in a slightly mocking tone. My ears perked up; my mother never prepared anything plain. Unpacking the groceries, she waved a box at me and said, "I even bought 'Bisto' – it's a gravy powder you add to the stew."

As Mummy stirred, she mocked her brother-in-law's preference for plain food. "You see, Mariam, this is plain food. I hope you like it!"

I just listened. Actually, the stew smelled good. But I decided not to say anything.

The plain beef stew was a hit with her sister and brother-in-law but also with us. There was none left at the end of the evening. Mummy couldn't understand why we liked it. I don't think she ever made that beef stew ever again and for all I know the box of Bisto probably ended up in the garbage. For my mother, cooking with Bisto was just one step above opening a can of Chef Boyardee. Yet my mother regularly served us 'plain' food such as hamburgers, meat loaf, and fish sticks, although she always had a variety of mustards, chutneys, and other accompaniments to add taste. Thinking back, I believe that what she was offended by was the implication that there was something foreign about her style of cooking.

My mother's letters often described special family meals to her friends and family. Reading them decades later confirms the high status that food had in our household. In 1959 my mother wrote to a good friend thanking her for sending a Ukrainian cookbook as a Christmas gift. She explained that she had made honey cake, but it was not as good as her mother's. Speaking of my father she wrote: "I am fortunate that Din (referring to my father) likes food experimentation and tries the dishes which are already familiar to me. My sister's husband dislikes 'all that foreign stuff' – an attitude I abhor." Twenty years later she wrote about the birthday dinner that my fifteen-year-old sister and I (then twenty) had made for her: shrimp salad, roasted chicken, celery salad, and layer cake for dessert. Papa made fresh rolls to accompany the dinner.

Later the same year, I made Christmas dinner. According to my mother's letters I told my family that they had to dress up: "No pyjamas and dressing gowns"! We started with champagne cocktails and Parmesan twists in the living room. Dinner was homemade beef consommé, roasted turkey with dressing and gravy, baked tomato stuffed with spinach, rolls made by my father, and a choice of two desserts – cranberry pie or crème caramel. I must have cooked for several days. Until I read these letters, I'd completely forgotten just how much effort I put into those family meals. My favourite cookbook at the time was the *New York Times Cookbook*. I especially enjoyed making classic desserts like *génoise*, *profiteroles*, and *bûche de Noël*. While my repertory of holiday dinners has expanded to include Passover and *Eid*, I still make recipes that I made as a teenager.

Four cooks don't spoil the broth

My mother cooked from Monday to Friday. On Saturdays and Sundays my father took over the kitchen. Every weekend for more than half a century, Papa cooked Pakistani food and baked bread for his family.

As children, we were encouraged to try new and exotic flavours and began learning to cook as soon as we could reach the kitchen counter. As teenagers, my sister and I were expected to make the family dinner once a week. At first, our mother would supervise, but before long this was no longer necessary. I really enjoyed planning the menu. I would spend hours poring over cookbooks only to have my choice of recipe vetoed by Mummy. "It's too elaborate," she would say, or "You can't serve shrimp for a weeknight dinner – it's just too expensive. I want you to know how to cook tasty, economical food."

I went along, sure that I would never ever make meatloaf when I finally had my own place. The lessons learned in my parents' kitchen paid off as I have fed others and myself for decades, sometimes on a shoestring budget. My meatloaf is pretty good.

Some of the meals I made were utter disasters. I remember presenting my family with a beef and Bing cherry dish. Even as I was cooking, it smelled like a foul cross between a hamburger and dessert. It was awful. My parents gamely ate, it although my mother told me diplomatically that it was not a recipe worth repeating. We were encouraged not to be afraid to try something new. When my sister's grade one class put together a recipe book as a Mother's Day project, she thought it was perfectly normal to submit, as her contribution, a recipe for French onion soup from the *New York Times Cookbook*! She came home from school bawling because the other children had made fun of her. They had never heard of onion soup. But this was only a temporary setback. By high school she was cooking *à la* Julia Child.

On Saturday afternoons, before she learned to drive, Mummy would go downtown. She would get dressed up and walk to the corner where she took the number sixteen bus downtown. Papa cooked and looked after us for the whole afternoon. He would teach us how to measure the spices or how to wash vegetables and the right amount of water to add to rice.

The format of Papa's cooking rarely varied. It was as predictable as a Sunday sermon. He would make some kind of curry from beef, chicken, lamb, or fish and then a vegetable or lentil dish. Initially, rice was always served but as his cooking skills improved, he became adept at making *chapatis* or *naan*. My mother made a salad – usually cucumber mixed with yogurt or sliced tomatoes with lime.

Once in our teens, my sister and I took over making the salad. Now, in my own house, I follow the same format whenever I cook Pakistani food.

There were always new recipes to try. Mid-week, my parents would sit at the kitchen table, drinking their morning, milky tea and discussing what to make for dinner that weekend. Would it be the tried-and-true *khatta ghosht* (sour meat) – a dish of beef, tomatoes, onions, and garlic, cooked for hours over a slow flame – that they had adapted from a recipe in the *Pakistan Times* many years ago? Or how about the recipe for Bengali-style shrimp in last weekend's *New York Times* magazine?

"I had the most marvellous dish in Lahore," reminisced my mother after returning from a trip to Pakistan in the early 1970s. "Lamb and turnips – the dish is called *shabdaig*.

"It was so magnificent that I asked the cook to make it again and sat in the kitchen watching and taking notes. The turnips became soft but never mushy after simmering all day."

Holding a spoon in one hand, Mummy put the lid on the pot of *shabdaig* simmering on the stove and shook her head. "It just doesn't taste the same." Despite her many attempts to replicate this recipe, it was never as delicious as she remembered it.

"Absolutely not. I will not skim the fat off the top of the *daal* – it's full of flavour. How many times do I have to tell you?" Papa slammed the lid back onto the pot and looked at my mother defiantly. In his mind, what my mother was asking was sacrilegious. When the leftover food had chilled in the refrigerator, and Papa was downstairs watching television or in his office, Mummy would spoon off the red or yellow tinted fat that had settled at the top. As she would be the one reheating the leftovers for dinner the next day my father was none the wiser.

It took years for Papa to agree to use less fat and salt in his dishes. Eventually, high blood pressure and cholesterol forced him to. His cooking style, learned from his mother, involved starting at the highest heat possible, and never changed over the years. He left behind a trail of charred pots and pans. The worst was when Papa would make *namkeen chai*, a salty milky tea enjoyed by Kashmiris. The taste is unique. For me, the salt totally overpowered any tea taste. Preparing this tea involves bringing a mixture of milk, salt, and green tea leaves to a rolling boil. Anyone who has ever boiled milk will know what a mess it leaves behind. Eventually Mummy told Papa that he could only make *namkeen chai* in a beat-up pot that she got at the Salvation

Army for five cents. When the knob on the lid fell off my father replaced it with a scrap piece of wood.

Perhaps to compensate for what he did to pots, Papa was a fantastic dishwasher. As a struggling PhD student in Montréal, he took a job washing dishes when his fellowship money ran out. When he cooked, he always cleaned up the kitchen afterwards. My mother's friends were envious – not only did my mother never cook on weekends, but she didn't need to clean up after her husband. Papa was smug about his dishwashing skills. Scowling, shaking his head, and muttering, "How disgusting!" under his breath he would inspect the dishes my sister and I washed, pointing out any stains we had missed with his index finger.

Mr. Dhariwal

In 1960s Canada it was a challenge to find the ingredients for Pakistani food. At the end of visits to Pakistan, spices were stuffed into every crevice of our family's suitcases. In Victoria, my mother scoured grocery stores, occasionally announcing that she had found a long-searched-for ingredient in a dusty corner of an obscure market. Whole cardamom!! Fresh chillies were but a dream. And who in Canada had heard of basmati rice in 1966? After some experimentation, Papa concluded that Uncle Ben's rice was the best. He longed for the special flour that he needed to make authentic tasting *chapattis* and *naan*.

A wave of immigrants from South Asia to Canada in the 1970s and 1980s created a demand for grocery items typically used in Indian and Pakistani cuisine. Papa checked out each new store in Victoria. A small store run by a Sikh family became his favourite haunt and he would go there every weekend with the excuse that he needed to buy one thing or another. I think what he really wanted to do was to speak Punjabi again.

Over time, Papa befriended the owner, Mr. Dhariwal, a stunning, tall Sikh man who was always impeccably dressed in a turban that complemented his outfit. We were invited to the Dhariwals' house for dinner. Mr. Dhariwal told us that he had been part of the guard assigned to Lord Mountbatten, the last Viceroy of India. He showed us a 1940s photograph of himself in uniform and then he disappeared for a few minutes, only to reappear, totally impressive, dressed in his 1947 livery complete with matching turban and feather. Mr. Dhariwal was extremely proud that his uniform still fit him perfectly.

Returning from a trip to Mr. Dhariwal's store, Papa would be giddy with anticipation as he unpacked the bag of purchases, placing them on the kitchen table for all of us to see.

"Look at this!" he would say, pointing excitedly at the jars of *achar* – or pickles – made of lemon, lime, mango, or carrots and swirling with orangey oil and huge chillies. Their flavour was powerful even with the jar still closed. There were lentils of all colours – red, yellow, green, black. Huge bags of spices – fenugreek, cardamom, coriander, cumin, and turmeric, all with such strong aromas that my father packed them in plastic bags inside old dill pickle jars to keep them from cross-contaminating each other. Papa dug deep into his recipe collection for inspiration to find out what to do with these new ingredients. There was also rice from

Amritsar, India in a burlap sack. He recognized the address on the bag. After the rice was finished, he saved the bag and kept it in his study, filled with rubber bands.

Eating out

Our family usually ate at home. This was common in 1960s and '70s Canada before two-career couples and the swelling numbers of families eating at restaurants. Going to restaurants was something we did on vacation. Part of the reason for this was that the selection of restaurants in Victoria was, as my mother used to say, not very electrifying. Restaurant cuisine in 1960s and '70s Victoria was primarily pre-immigration British. It was almost as if establishments such as the Empress Hotel, Holyrood House, the Tudor Room at the Oak Bay Beach Hotel, and the McPherson Theatre Restaurant shared a giant kitchen and a chef. Their menus were limited to British classics such as roast beef and Yorkshire pudding, steak and kidney pie, roast chicken, or grilled fish. And there were always green peas. Dessert was trifle or crème caramel. Yawn.

With their sophisticated palates and constrained by the demands and costs of raising a family, my parents rarely ate out in Victoria. But every so often we would have take-out food on a Friday night. There were three options: Chinese, pizza, or fish and chips. These were big events. My sister and I would fight over which one of us would accompany Papa to go and pick up our dinner. This was followed by the excruciating drive home in a car smelling of the food that would soon be on the table. Fish and chips were wrapped in plain newsprint, the Chinese food was in cardboard containers, and pizza came in a huge box. I loved opening the packages and how their contents permeated the whole house. Chinese food was particularly fun because of the small packets of sesame seeds, soy sauce, and chilli sauce that were included with our order.

There were the restaurant meals, usually in Vancouver and Seattle, where my parents used to go several times a year to get away from Victoria. Having a good meal or two was usually the highlight of the trip. Many day trips to Vancouver were anchored by lunch at the Hotel Vancouver's Spanish Grill, a family favourite where we had wonderful meals.

We were taught that cocktails always prefaced a nice meal – a very dry martini for my father and a daiquiri for my mother. Shirley Temples for the girls. Over the years, we learned how to order in a restaurant, how to behave, and all about tipping. "Ten percent at lunch and fifteen percent at dinner; more if the service is superb," my father would say.

Family recipes

The summer I was fourteen, too young to have a job but too old to spend my days playing, my mother had a great idea. I was moping around the house, bored and driving her nuts.

"I've got just the job for you," said my mother brightly, "and I'll pay you to do it." She smiled at me, waiting for my reaction.

"What?" was my sullen and flat adolescent reply.

"I want you to type out all the recipes for Pakistani food. They really are a big mess – newspaper clippings, pieces of scrap paper. You can practice your typing and earn a little bit of money to spend on vacation. How about it?"

Since I had nothing else to do, I agreed to type out the recipes. My mother had a portable manual typewriter that I set up at my desk. Over the next few weeks, I went through the stack of family recipes for Pakistani food and typed them onto index cards. I'm not sure how many of these cards I typed up – probably about two or three dozen.

When I left home for university, my mother made me photocopies of all the recipe cards – I still have them. I don't make Pakistani food often. But when I do, I always plan my menu by leafing through these recipes. Some of the cards have notations in my mother's or my father's handwriting. Like the recipe for *dal* – a scrawl in Papa's hand advises that the amount of lentils and water used can be reduced in equal proportions.

As I look through the recipes, I remember my father standing at the stove as the scent of turmeric and coriander spread throughout the house like incense. Bengali fish – I can almost smell the bright yellow sauce and taste the crunchy red onions and the tender fish. If I close my eyes, I can feel the contrast of the fresh dill and perfectly cooked shrimp blending with the delicate taste of basmati rice in my mouth. Or smell the fragrant scent of cinnamon bark that my father has dropped into the pot of rice that is simmering on the back burner.

مریم

It is a Saturday afternoon. I hear the front door open and close. My mother, just back from downtown, goes immediately to the kitchen, still in her coat. All four burners on the stove are on. Stopping at the altar, she lifts up each pot lid and takes a deep whiff of each one, savouring the escaping aromas. Smiling, she goes to take off her coat, knowing that a wonderful meal awaits her.

مريم

Like all parents, mine passed on their special knowledge and traditions. The most precious of these was the gift of food. This gift was multi-faceted – it included an appreciation for different tastes, a keen sense of culinary adventure, curiosity, and development of the confidence and skills I have drawn upon and honed to feed myself and those I love throughout my life. The gift of food is there when I make a pot of soup with whatever's left in the refrigerator and also when I look through the family recipes while planning a special meal. It is an obligation to eat well. The gift of food is an attitude, rooted in the pleasures our family shared together so long ago. It is memory, of my life with my parents. It is emotion, as I recall the feelings food evoked at our family meals and mourn my parents, now deceased. It is sustenance that maintains not only my life and my passions but keeps me connected to where I came from. It is the curiosity to try new dishes and new cuisines and the pleasure I take when I share food with my family and friends.

When I pray at the altar of food, I give thanks for the gift of food. Amen.

10

Our Heinz Ketchup House

2444 Alpine Crescent, Victoria, 1966

Mummy opened the door of her new house. Two women beamed at her. One of them held out a yellow Pyrex dish.

"Good morning, I'm Margo MacDowell." She turned slightly and pointed behind her. "That's my house – the yellow one – diagonally across from you."

"And I'm Jane Edwards! I live just next door – across that little fence over there." Jean waved her hand to the right. "We've brought you something to welcome you to the neighbourhood. Everybody loves tuna casserole!" Mummy cradled the warm dish between her hands.

"And I'm Catherine. Very nice of you to have dropped by. Would you like to come in?"

"Oh no, we just popped over for a minute. What we really wanted to ask you is if you're free tomorrow morning at ten to come to a coffee party at Jane's. Just girls!"

Catherine thought of the stacks of unpacked boxes and the mountains of things to be put away. It was only morning and she was already exhausted. She didn't have time for coffee and gossip with a bunch of suburban housewives. Before she could stop herself, the words tumbled out of her mouth.

"Margo, Jane, it's very kind of you. But I'm up to my ears. So much to do! And you know, I'm not really a coffee party girl." Mummy smiled weakly. "Another time?"

Looking surprised, the welcome wagon said goodbye and Mummy went upstairs with the tuna casserole. They hadn't anticipated my mother's "coffee party girl" reply.

Decades later, talking about this incident with my father, he was still perplexed. "What on earth was she thinking?"

It was only when I read my mother's letters written to a lifelong friend that I finally understood why my mother acted the way she did. Raising two young children, she felt isolated and alone in Victoria and still missed Montréal keenly. The year before we moved, in 1965, she wrote her friend saying that she had wasted her life. Mummy craved solitude, time to read and write, and dreamt of a career. It is telling that in a collection of letters written by my mother to her dear friend that span more than a quarter century, the only year where my mother never wrote was 1966, the year my parents bought their house.

The ladies of Alpine Crescent gave Mummy a second chance. Although sipping coffee from a china cup and talking about cooking and children was not her idea of a good time, she didn't show it. Eyeing the hostesses' wedding china and silver tea set proudly on display in a glass-fronted buffet, Mummy knew she had little in common with "the girls." She was interested in China, not china, and she put books on display, not her tableware.

"It was an utter waste of a morning. That new book by Malcolm X had arrived a few days earlier and I was dying to read it. Instead, there I was, talking drivel," Mummy told me, years later.

The "girls" were all from Western Canada. Mummy tried to find common ground with them. Did they like the new Canadian flag? Were they excited about Expo 67? They bemoaned the replacement of the old Red Ensign flag with the maple leaf, could not understand why French-Canadians didn't all just learn English, and had no interest in going to Expo the following year.

مریم

Alpine Crescent was developed in the mid-1950s. By the start of the '60s, all of the lots on the Crescent had houses on them except for an awkward patch of land with a big granite rock in the middle. Nobody wanted to buy it. A local builder acquired the land at a bargain price, divided it and built two houses. The more attractive one, 2446, was purchased, but 2444, where half of the back yard was rock, languished unsold for a long time.

Situated on a wedge of land shaped like a longish piece of pie, the backyard resembled a moonscape, dominated by a huge granite rock formation and debris thrown there by the neighbours.

My parents moved to Victoria in the late summer of 1961. The owners of our rental house were returning to town early in 1966 so the Pals had two months to find a new home. It was Christmas 1965, and I was in grade two. I did not want to move. I had made friends with the neighbours; spending hours with Mrs. Battersby making plum jam or curing smoked salmon with Mr. Edworthy next door.

"Din, we should buy something in Oak Bay," Mummy told Papa over their morning tea. My father didn't reply. Papa was not so sure. He associated the purchase of a house with permanency: not just Canada but Victoria. He realized his wife was right, but he was still several years away from openly admitting that she was far savvier than he was in such matters. So he insisted that the new house be near my school, to spare me from changing schools, and that it not have a steep driveway. The area around my school was hilly so steep driveways were the norm. As for my feelings on changing schools, I was more upset that I wasn't allowed to go out for Halloween! Papa was very concerned about snow in Canada's most temperate city and the impact of a new school on me. These odd arguments were my father's attempt to make it difficult to find a house, thus avoiding the commitment that buying a house entailed.

The only house that fit his exacting criteria was the one on Alpine Crescent. It had a gently sloped driveway and was close to my school. My mother disliked it immediately. My father, preoccupied with being a full-time university professor and President of the University Faculty Association, had limited time and patience for house hunting. Of course, they bought it.

Melancholy and forlorn, 2444 Alpine Crescent occupied a treeless lot with a patch of weeds and dead branches where there should have been a lush, green front lawn. The house desperately needed love.

Reached by a staircase from the front door, the main living space, living and dining rooms, large sundeck, kitchen, three bedrooms, and one and a half bathrooms were on the upper floor. There was also an unfinished basement and a two-car garage. It was not a well-built house and inexpensive materials had been used throughout. "Several days after we moved into the house I looked up and realized that all the ceilings were finished with cheap tiles," observed my mother.

The top half of the boxy house was covered in white stucco and the bottom encased in wood siding. Ornamental shutters flanked the windows. As a final flourish, the contractor installed bizarre decorations on the white wall just above the painted wood siding. These consisted of a square-shaped piece of wood about one foot high. The square was turned sideways to resemble a diamond and was bisected by three long horizontal pieces of wood through the top, middle, and bottom. This decoration, the fake shutters, and the wood siding were all painted in a surreal coral colour immediately christened by my father as "Heinz Ketchup." It didn't take long for my parents to remove the wall embellishments and repaint the sidings and shutters in a soft shade of gray. The Heinz Ketchup paint colour always symbolized, for my father, how hard he had worked to improve the house.

For years, the neighbours threw their garbage into what would become our back yard. Garbage pickup was infrequent, and the dump was far away. Old tires, empty paint cans, broken furniture, and other junk was strewn where there should have been emerald-green grass, a swing set, and laundry drying in the breeze. Not too long after we set up house, a crash from the backyard pierced the evening silence as we ate dinner. By the time Papa and his flashlight got to the back door all he could see was a shadowy figure slipping over the back fence. In the morning light we saw that fresh rubbish had been added to the collection. My parents wondered if this same lack of respect would have been shown to a white family. The landscaper my parents hired had to haul away a couple of truckloads of their neighbours' debris before he could see the ground. Effectively, my parents paid to have Alpine Crescent's junk removed.

Alpine Crescent was a solidly middle-class neighbour-hood. It was safe and there were kids everywhere. There was hourly bus service to downtown Victoria and a red mailbox stood at the corner. Air-raid sirens installed during World War II were tested regularly. Some people still talked about the threat of the "Japs" invading.

Alpine Crescent was well situated. It was close to Frank Hobbs Elementary School where I completed grades one to seven, graduating with the Citizenship prize in 1971. A junior and senior high were a few minutes further away. The ocean was close enough that I could hear the ships' foghorns in the Strait of Juan de Fuca blowing on winter nights from my bed.

In the other direction was a modest outdoor strip mall with a Shop Easy grocery store and a gas station/garage, variety store, bank, and post office. Mummy used to buy her aerogrammes there until she overheard the clerk whispering something derogatory to his colleague about her regular letters to Pakistan. There was a butcher, Wakeham's, and a convenience store that everybody (except us) called the "Chink" store. Up the hill was the growing campus of the new University of Victoria where my father taught. There was also a convent, surrounded by woods and accessible by a long dark driveway where, much to my surprise, a distant missionary nun cousin of my mother's stayed when visiting Victoria in the early 1970s.

Like most of Victoria, BC, Alpine Crescent's inhabitants were of British ancestry, and this was reflected in the names of our neighbours – Edwards, Cooper, MacDowell, McMichael. In 1966 Victoria, "immigrant" meant coming from Britain or maybe Northern Europe.

The last two houses built on Alpine Crescent, located on the worst lots, were both purchased by mixed couples. My parents, a Pakistani man and a Polish-Canadian woman, and our neighbours, who were Dutch-Indonesian immigrants, somehow settled down next door to each other. It was an absurd coincidence.

Both houses had taken a while to sell. It's as if Canadians knew the houses were trouble. Our house, 2444, seemed like a house that was doomed from the start – its yard used as a garbage dump, rejected by countless buyers, and located on a rocky, awkwardly shaped lot.

The Soehartos – Hans, Elizabeth, Joyce, and Patty, lived next door to us. Although they had lived there for a couple of years when we moved in, their house was only slightly less sad than ours. No flowers had been planted and the backyard was dark with too many trees. Hans, from Holland (although his surname was Dutch-Indonesian), was in insurance. Mrs. Soeharto, his Indonesian, mini-skirted wife, was slim and petite and had long, curly black hair that she often wore in a ponytail.

Papa was pleasantly surprised to have them living next door. The two families got along relatively well. The first summer we lived on Alpine Crescent, eight-year-old me followed Joyce and Patty around like a puppy. I loved being with the older girls. We'd listen to "Downtown" or "Don't Sleep in the Subway" again and again. Or put on one of their Herb Alpert records and dance like maniacs.

On the other side lived the Edwards family, John and Jane, and their teenage girl and boy. John owned Edwards Tires downtown. John was a big guy and his wife, Jane, always looked picture perfect, driving her red convertible that her husband had delivered on Christmas Day with a huge bow on it. Mr. Edwards gave discounts on tires to some of the neighbours, but never to my father or Mr. Soeharto.

Across the street were Margo and Jay MacDowell, originally from Saskatchewan. Mr. MacDowell was in the Navy until he was diagnosed with multiple sclerosis and stopped working. His wife went back to work as a nurse. My mother admired her because she had a profession. I remember her telling me that a woman should always have something to fall back on because you never know what can happen to your husband. She and Margo got on reasonably well until we went away to Montréal for a year. The house was rented, and Margo was asked to keep an eye on things. Margo was a forthright and blunt person, and my parents were sure that if anything happened, she would let them know. After a year away, our family returned to discover considerable damage to the house. They also heard stories from neighbours about some of the goings-on. For reasons that were never explained, Margo kept her mouth shut and didn't tell my parents a thing. They never really trusted her after that, and the friendship sputtered and died.

I was constantly over at the MacDowells'. Their eldest, Kay, was a year younger than me. Their house was a going concern. There was always something happening, especially in summer. They had a huge garden, many fruit trees, and they canned and froze food all summer long. The kids were recruited to help and so was I.

At Christmas, Mr. MacDowell put up a crèche outside their front door and fixed up a portable record player that played religious Christmas music every evening and all day on December 25. I used to think it was the greatest Christmas decoration ever.

Mr. and Mrs. Cooper's place faced ours. Both clerks at Eaton's, their four kids were all in high school or older. Tom loved to come over and talk to my father about political theory and he was constantly borrowing books from us. Mr. Cooper used to charge backwards in his car out of his driveway without looking and one day he crashed into my father's car. He lied to the insurance company and said he had honked. I was too young to know all the details, but I think my father, tired of fighting, chose not to dispute Mr. Cooper's claim. He was hoping to avoid yet another deep-freeze with an Alpine Crescent resident. Nonetheless, this caused lingering tension between the two households.

Mr. Haultin, the ultimate handyman, lived next to the Coopers. By day, he was a vocational teacher at a local high school. Evenings and weekends were spent in his back yard building a twenty-five-foot sailboat. Alpine Crescent was fed up with the noise of his whiny sander and the sickly-sweet smell of fiberglass wafting into our houses in the evenings. Once when I was very sick, the constant din from the Haultin house stopped me from sleeping. My distraught mother knocked on their door and pleaded for quiet but the cacophony continued. As she noted dryly, the only thing that tore him away from his sailboat was a leopard-bikinied Mrs. Soeharto mowing the lawn!

A crane was needed to lift the finished sailboat out of the backyard, over the roof, and onto the back of a special flatbed truck. The whole neighbourhood turned out to watch.

"Look!" said Mummy, pointing to the boat as we watched the spectacle from our living room window. "He's named that bloody boat 'The Arrogant'!"

"What does arrogant mean?" I asked. I was ten years old.

A few months later, Mr. Haultin put his place up for sale and he and his family moved away. The kids on Alpine Crescent were sure they had sailed to Hawaii, never to return.

The other neighbours included the Duchamps, a British car mechanic with a French name whose family car was a 1920s Rolls Royce found in a barn and refurbished.

Across from the Duchamps lived a middle-aged schoolteacher known as Miss Marquette whose two adopted, disabled children I would occasionally babysit. A door or two down the Crescent lived the Taylors, from England. Mr. Taylor, a naval pilot for foreign ships passing through the treacherous Strait of Juan de Fuca, had a wee dram too much one night and ran his ship aground.

Redheaded twin brothers Ron and Adam were down the street. Both sons got their BAs to please their British immigrant father who did not have the opportunity to get an education. Then they got jobs with the BC government and each bought a TR6 sports car to get to work.

We moved into the house on February 1, 1966. Except for the coffee party invitation, there didn't seem to be much neighbourliness on Alpine Crescent. My mother found it strange.

"When we moved to Alpine Crescent, we had already lived in Victoria for five years," she said once. "We didn't expect to be greeted with kisses, but elsewhere we rented in

Victoria, people came to say hello when they saw the moving van. But on Alpine Crescent I saw the neighbours looking from behind their curtains. I felt like I was being watched. It was bizarre. Back then I couldn't drive, and I remember walking to the corner to take the bus downtown when we'd only been in the house a few days. Nobody said 'hello'."

Victoria is not a very friendly place. There's a certain reserve and people stick to themselves. My parents moved to Alpine Crescent from a house on nearby MacDonald Drive, just five minutes away. There, they made lifelong friendships. My father got along well with the men of MacDonald Drive who were not very different than those on Alpine Crescent: salesmen, insurance agents, and construction workers.

As spring turned into summer, my parents couldn't help but notice that the neighbours were all friends with each other. Mr. Edwards, Mr. MacDowell, and Mr. Cooper would gather in one of their backyards for a beer. Various families strolled over to each other's houses for summer barbecues. But the inhabitants of the last two homes to be built on Alpine Crescent, where the immigrants lived, were never included. Eating dinner on our sundeck, we could hear the laughter coming from one of the nearby backyards where our neighbours had gathered. When a retired British couple moved into a smaller house up the Crescent, they seemed to be invited everywhere.

Apart from the Pals and the Soehartos, Alpine Crescent was home to other immigrants but only from Britain. South Asians were rare in Canada, thanks to racist immigration policies that kept them out until 1947. A quota existed on immigrants from Pakistan and India from 1951 until 1961. Perhaps the neighbours found it difficult to accept that a brown man married to a white woman had moved next door. And that he taught at the university.

Papa didn't have much in common with Alpine Crescent's men. He didn't like football or hockey, hadn't fought in Korea or World War II, and thought the Shriners were racist and silly. It did not help matters that my parents did not give out Halloween candy and ours was the only home without Christmas lights. But the coolness was there from the start, months before children would be fruitlessly ringing our doorbell on October 31, or our house, unembellished by Christmas lights, faded into the winter darkness.

In the summer of 1966, things started to fall apart. It started with a fence and a conscientious landscaper.

Mr. Klimoff, hired by my parents to bring some semblance of order and greenness to our pathetic yard, was suspicious. He wanted to put up a hedge parallel to the fence on the Edwards' side. This fence was constructed, he learned, just after the house was sold, and was completed before we moved in. Fences are not common in that part of Victoria.

Papa speculated about the fence, "Did they know that the new family moving in was not lily white?" He suspected that they did, and that that was why they built the fence. We'll never know for sure.

A surveyor was called to verify the property line. He showed my parents where a metal stake buried in the ground marked the border between the two yards. The fence was three feet inside my parents' property and had been built without the necessary permit. John Edwards, who lived next door and whose wife, Jane, had been part of the tuna casserole welcome wagon, had put up the fence. My parents were appalled and furious.

I overheard my parents talking about what the surveyor had found.

"Bunch of bastards," said my father. "Trying to take extra land. Disgusting. Absolutely disgusting." It was early morning, and my parents were talking in bed. Then my mother's voice:

"There's no way to raise this without causing tensions. It was done deliberately, and they thought nobody would notice. That fence should be torn down."

In the fall, my parents finally decided to speak to John and Jane about the offending fence. The conversation did not go well. Our neighbour simply refused to acknowledge the encroachment, even after a second survey that he himself arranged and paid for also showed that he was in the wrong.

John accused my father of being "too sensitive," "not neighbourly," and helpfully suggested that my father did not know "how things are done here." Papa replied it was not a question of sensitivity or neighbourliness but rather a simple respect for legal boundaries. After this, Mr. Edwards and his wife stopped saying hello to us. My parents, after considering the options available, including going to court, decided to live with the fence.

A few years later, the Edwards proposed building a back deck off their kitchen. This time they applied for a permit for their project. If approved, they could have quaffed beer just ten feet away from my parents' bedroom window. My parents objected and the deck proposal was rejected. The Cold War with the Edwards family took on glacial proportions.

A year after they moved in, my parents decided to build a fence on the other side of the property, between the Soehartos' yard and ours. What I think happened next is that Mrs. Soeharto argued that a fence should be a collaborative effort between neighbours. Her interpretation of my parents putting up the fence was that it was somehow an insult personally directed towards her and her family. In her mind, the only reason we wanted the fence was because her family were not good neighbours. This was not true; my father wanted the fence to delineate the yard.

Nothing my parents said to her to explain their rationale had any impact. She was highly emotional. I have vague memories of a shouting match between Mr. and Mrs. Soeharto and my father. A year later the Soehartos sold their house. Through online research, I learned that Mr. Soeharto died recently and that, sadly, he was predeceased by one of his daughters.

Many years later, I remember that my mother explained to me why my father wanted the yard fenced in. "He was used to a house being private, including the yard. That is how houses are designed in Pakistan."

But, I thought, he lived in Canada! Papa had paid a high price for his fence.

An Anglo-Indian couple, the Ghoshes, bought the Soeharto place. Mr. Ghosh was from somewhere in southern India and his wife, Sally, was British. In a white town like Victoria, what are the odds that two of the handful of South

Asian mixed couples in town would end up living side-by-side on Alpine Crescent? But that is exactly what happened.

My parents tried to welcome the Ghoshes. Their efforts fell flat. Mr. Ghosh seemed very ill at ease around my father. Even though I was a self-absorbed teenager and not very perceptive when it came to the adults around me, I remember noticing how awkward he was.

Years later, when I got to know South Asia much better, I realized it was a cultural issue – Mr. Ghosh, a Hindu, felt very uncomfortable around my father, a well-educated urban Muslim. My father speculated that Mr. Ghosh came from a very poor background, but that he had excelled in his studies, been awarded scholarships, and left India to pursue a graduate degree.

The Ghoshes came to Victoria from Toronto. At the time, Toronto was adjusting to an influx of South Asian immigrants and racist incidents were widely reported in the press. When Papa asked Mr. Ghosh about his own experiences in Toronto, the immediate and vociferous denial that there was any discrimination or racism rang hollow with my father. He was sure that his new neighbour was not telling the truth. Mr. Ghosh sensed this.

مریم

I lost touch with everyone on Alpine Crescent years ago. When I started writing about the neighbourhood I grew up in, I contacted the occupants of 2444, told them who I was, and asked to see some photos of what the house looks like now. The new owner graciously replied and sent me some photos. I was excited when I wrote back to thank them. I made the mistake of sharing some anecdotes about my childhood. The reply was polite and distant. I had forgotten about the coolness of people in Victoria.

مریم

What happened to us on Alpine Crescent? Was it race? Was it class? Was it both? For whatever reason, the people of Alpine Crescent did not make my family feel welcome and wanted in the neighbourhood. I looked at our house on Google maps and saw that, more than half a century later, the illegal fence still stands. What was the motivation for Mr. Edwards putting up that fence in a neighbourhood where nobody had them? Who had the gall to dump their junk into our backyard knowing our family had just moved in? All these years later I don't know. I never will. As a child, I went to school and played on Alpine Crescent with the other kids. It was my world. Yet even then I sensed that the neighbours treated us like we were different.

When I was twenty years old, I left the Heinz Ketchup house and moved to Montréal.

مریم

It was a cloudy, humid, late July afternoon at the hotel pool in Dhaka, Bangladesh. I had just climbed out of the shallow end and wrapped myself in a towel. I heard bells ringing and turned to look. A young man in a smart uniform was waving a belled sign; my name was written on a little chalkboard. I waved to him.

"That's for me," I said. The young man smiled at me and nodded. He motioned to the pool attendant who picked up a telephone on an astoundingly long cord and placed it on the table next to me. He picked up the receiver and handed it to me.

"Hello?" I said, throwing my voice into what sounded like a tunnel full of static.

"Hello, Mariam, how are you?" replied my father. His voice sounded strong despite the terrible line.

"Fine, Papa, what's happening?"

Through the din I heard my father clear his throat, a lifelong indication that he was about to say something big.

"Well, Mariam, I've put the house up for sale."

"What?" I said. "But Papa, you just retired last month. Too much change isn't good."

I heard more static, some squeaking, and then the line went dead. I put down the receiver. There was no point in calling back.

I looked at the pool. It was so inviting. I dove back in and swam some more to clear my head.

More than a year had passed since I had been to my family home in Victoria. At thirty-one, I was five years into a demanding career in international development. In 1989, I spent four months working in Senegal, followed by a week in Rome. And now Bangladesh. It seemed that there was never time to go back to Victoria anymore. Papa was often in Montréal and that Christmas I met him and my sister in Pakistan where we spent two weeks together. Since my mother died two years earlier, the house didn't seem the same. Papa didn't keep the tin on the top shelf of the kitchen cupboard full of little hard candies or top up the baking supplies. I felt a bit lost whenever I came home. I didn't know many of the new people on the street and the old ones, like Mr. Edwards, never greeted me anyway.

When I came out of the pool I felt better. Selling the house was part of the natural order of things. I had a few boxes of books in the basement but other than that my life was in Montréal. But on the long flight home from Hong Kong to New York I woke up from a deep sleep somewhere over the Pacific. All I could think about was the house. I felt a sob convulse through my body and before I knew it, I was crying. Our Heinz Ketchup house was no more.

II

Pakistani Handyman

Papa, 1972

Siraj-ud-Din Pal put the stack of photographs on the table. He looked at his youngest son and said, "Very impressive. But my dear *Izzmia*, why do you insist on living in a country where you have to exhaust yourself? Now I see why I never get any letters from you."

Papa sighed softly, not wanting his father to hear, and picked the photographs up off the table. He put them into the envelope and then sat silently listening to his father talk.

"I should have known better," he thought to himself. But his father wasn't finished. Papa braced himself.

"*Izzmia*, you have lived abroad for almost twenty years now. Don't you think it's time for you to come home?"

Papa was silent. He had hoped that maybe his father would be interested to see all the work he had done on the house. He'd made himself a beautiful office in the basement, painted the outside of the house, and made dozens of improvements. A one-year fellowship had turned into a life in Canada with a Canadian wife, two children, and a house that always needed maintenance or repair. Yet his father kept insisting, as usual, that he should come home. Would he ever understand that Pakistan had nothing to offer him?

Big Uncle had the same attitude when he came to visit Canada from Pakistan a few years earlier. Sitting in the living room, drinking morning tea with my parents, he reacted to the tour of the house that his younger brother had just taken him on.

"But *Izzmia*, what I cannot understand is why it is necessary for you to spend so much of your own time on this renovation business. Is labour in Canada that expensive? An educated man does not belong in the basement hammering nails."

Papa and Mummy listened, smiles on their faces. Big Uncle continued, "Now I understand why you take so long to reply to my letters. You don't have any time."

My uncle and my grandfather came from another world. For them, the idea of an educated person performing manual labour was preposterous. Perhaps my father had the same attitude when he arrived in Canada, but by the time I was a young girl he had turned into an avid handyman. Papa adapted and adopted the motto of suburban Canada – "Do it yourself!"

Papa never lifted a finger growing up in Pakistan. He didn't need to cook, mow the lawn, or hang a picture. Yet in Canada, he became a terrific chef, an excellent gardener, and a very good handyman. He befriended staff at local home improvement stores and amassed a library of related books. The 1960s and 1970s were the heyday of the Time-Life book series. My father collected them all. He had a set on gardening, another one on home improvement, and a tome on automobile maintenance and repair.

Papa's career as a handyman really took off when we moved into the house that my parents bought on Alpine Crescent in 1966. Working on weekends, he taught himself how to use a jig saw, power drill, and various other tools so that he could build a study for himself and a TV room for the family.

In Victoria, Friday night was the end of the workweek, but it was also the beginning of weekend work. Fridays at 5 p.m., the men of Alpine Crescent – insurance salesmen, school-teachers, bank managers, and one university professor – transformed into handymen, gardeners, and mechanics.

On Saturdays and Sundays, our small neighbourhood was full of action. The green lawns hissed in the background while shrubbery was trimmed, cars were washed and waxed, and power tools hummed to the beat of the latest home improvement. Residents of Victoria's wealthier neighbour-hoods had gardeners and caretakers but in the middle-class community where I grew up, fathers mowed lawns, finished basements, and changed their spark plugs.

Saturday morning Papa was up early, organizing weekend chores and projects. He was always on the go and made the other fathers on Alpine Crescent look like slackers. Mummy got tired just looking at him.

"For God's sake, can't we ever rest on the weekend?" she exclaimed.

My father ignored her; he went ahead and planned his projects. He would often say, "I'm doing this for you, not for me."

Mummy got drawn in – choosing the colour of the paint or advising on the type of tree that would best fit a particular corner of the yard. As the elder daughter, I was drafted for all sorts of chores both inside and outside. My father didn't understand the value of sitting and doing nothing nor did he appreciate that even as a teenager I needed time to relax. I used to dread weekends. Why couldn't I sleep in and hang out with my friends like other kids did? When I developed severe hay fever and other allergies around age fourteen or fifteen, I was very relieved to be removed from lawn mowing duty.

Papa put a lot of care into building his study in the basement. He installed teak grain paneling on the walls and carpets from Pakistan on the floor. Mummy made him curtains out of a brown-checked fabric. Papa also built himself a huge desk out of a door that he stained dark brown. He mounted this on top of a filing cabinet on one side, and on the other, a simple cupboard with a single door where he kept his stationery. A large black swivel executive chair was ordered from the Sears catalogue. Floor-to-ceiling bookshelves, stained the same dark brown as his desk, covered all four walls.

The family typewriter lived on a nearby table. It was a big old manual Remington machine on which my mother had typed my father's PhD thesis. I used to love typing on it, but Papa's study was out of bounds for my sister and me. If we needed to type a paper for school, we used our mother's old portable, either at the dining room table or on our desks in our rooms.

In one corner of the study, Papa positioned a huge, upholstered chair. It was big and deep, and the arms were wide enough to hold one of my notebooks. Mummy had it reupholstered in brown corduroy. He used to sit there in the evenings. There would be a pile of unmarked exams or term papers on the floor on the left side of the chair and a second pile of corrected ones on the right side. Ironing in the TV room next door, I could hear the flutter of paper in the air as each exam booklet or term paper sailed onto the pile.

I remember curling up in that chair while my father sat at his desk for my weekly Sunday school for Muslims lessons. Papa loved his study and spent many happy hours working and reading there. He was especially proud of the fluorescent light he had installed in the ceiling, as well as extra electric and telephone outlets.

Next door was the TV room where Papa had made a built-in sewing desk, cupboards, and a closet for out-of-season clothing.

Papa always had a new project. He constructed valance boxes to put above the curtains in the living and dining rooms. Extra shelving was added on either side of the sliding glass door between the dining room and the sundeck. My mother didn't like the open concept dining room. She wanted to surprise her guests, *Upstairs, Downstairs* style, by ushering them into a beautifully set dining room. So, my father constructed a wall between the living room and dining room, in the middle of which was a folding louvred door. Mummy would announce that dinner was ready by opening the door with a dramatic flourish.

Once the basement renovation was complete, my mother permanently banished the television downstairs. She felt the living room was better suited to conversation, reading, or listening to music. Papa missed watching the nightly news, which broadcast right around dinnertime. My parents reached a compromise; when Papa constructed the wall between the dining room and living room, he cut a window just large enough for a small portable television. It sat on a shelf built into the opening. The house rule was that this television was only to be used for watching the news. For the most part, this was generally the case. Exceptions were made for important events such as election night coverage, the resignation of Richard Nixon, or the Olympics.

Papa's household projects became increasingly ambitious. He built and installed drawers and cabinets in the main bathroom, erected a decorative fence and gate between the side lawns and the backyard, made an incinerator out of bricks, and even repaired the roof. An impressive arsenal of tools and supplies grew in the storage area that he built in the garage for such a purpose.

The projects inside the house were the most numerous and elaborate. Papa also became a good gardener and made many improvements to the outside of the house. He extended the entryway, added extra lights outside, and planted hedges, a rose garden, and many beautiful trees.

Mummy may have wanted quiet weekends, but she could not deny the value of Papa's skills. All she had to do was mention that she needed something, and it would be done. A fabulous spice rack for the kitchen. A tall narrow bookcase for her university books and materials. A special chrysanthemum bed in the garden.

My mother also made sure that my father knew how much she appreciated what he was doing even though she didn't really want to be part of it. She would bring him a cold beer while he was working or make him a sardine sandwich for lunch. It was her way of supporting him while not getting too involved or drawn in.

Though I am no handyman weekend warrior, I like to think that I know more about these things than the average chick. My father taught me to always use wall anchors, that latex paint was better, and how to stake tomatoes.

Twenty-three years after purchasing the house, just two years after my mother's tragic and early death, Papa retired and sold the house. It never occurred to me at the time, but now I wonder if he missed working around the house after all those years. I never thought to ask him. He saved many of his tools and a selection of what he used to call "useful things," like a device to unplug a drain – which he would occasionally, with reluctance, lend to me. In the last years of his life, he forgot that I had borrowed things from him. This is how I acquired his favourite gardening book and an avocado green plastic toolbox full of drill bits. Whenever I needed a particular size of screw, I would always go over to his condo and see if he had what I needed. He was always delighted if he did.

Papa's gardening skills were now put primarily to use tending to a garden on his condo balcony as well as maintaining a small flowerbed and tree on my mother's grave. When he started to find the drive to the cemetery too long, he asked me to take charge. We went there together. He taught me how to prune the tree that he had planted there many years before. Since then, I have planted flowers and maintained the tree at what is now my parents' grave.

My childhood of do-it-yourselfing profoundly influenced my approach to managing, maintaining, and repairing the various places I have lived throughout my life. I'm not the type of person who, when there's something to be done, looks for someone to do it. If it's not a particularly big or complicated job, I will tackle it myself. The Pakistani handyman, my father, cast a large shadow. For most of my life I naïvely assumed that most men were pretty handy. I do not pine for the hectic weekends of my youth, but maybe, for just a few days, it would be great to have a Pakistani handyman around.

12

Dinner at Helen's

Family picnic, 1976

I dreamt of junk food. I longed to eat a hamburger at the new McDonald's restaurant, but my mother refused to take me there. She disapproved of American fast foods, like Kentucky Fried Chicken, that were increasingly popular in Canada in the late 1960s. For Mummy, dinner out meant going to a proper restaurant like the dining room at the Empress Hotel, not to some burger joint. The cookies in my lunch were homemade; breakfast was hot cereal. Occasionally, Mummy would relent and let us have a treat such as a cake mix or a box of Cap'n Crunch.

When I was ten years old, my professor father went out of town to a conference. Helen, the American wife of one of his university colleagues, whose husband, Bob, was also attending the conference, invited my mother and my sister and me for a family dinner.

This was exciting! Helen's daughter was in my class and she always had Twinkies in her lunchbox. Sometimes she shared one with me. They were delicious. I prayed that they would serve Twinkies for dessert.

A few days later, since my mother didn't drive, Helen came to pick us up in her big wood panelled station wagon. As we stepped into the house I whispered to Mummy, "I don't smell any food."

"Shhh, be quiet!" she said.

Helen ushered us into the living room.

"Girls, would you like a soft drink? We have Coke and 7UP."

"Coke, please," I said. The three of us sat silently in the living room while our hostess went to the kitchen to fetch our drinks. I was having a good time already – at our house, my parents only allowed us to have soft drinks on birthdays and when our parents had guests over for dinner.

While Helen was out of the room, my mother gestured silently towards the empty dining table with her head – why wasn't it set for dinner? Later, back home, she said to us that she wondered if we were going out to a restaurant. Too polite to say anything, Mummy sat in the living room, making small talk with Helen's kids. Helen came back holding several bottles of Coke with straws bobbing in their necks. She handed me one. I took a long sip. It was so good!

A car pulled into the driveway. Its tires crackled on the gravel and then it stopped. The car door opened and closed. Footsteps. Then the doorbell rang. Helen jumped up and opened the door.

A delicious, greasy smell wafted into the living room.

"Mm, smells great!" I whispered to my mother.

"Shhh!" she replied.

The front door slammed shut. Helen came back into the living room, holding what looked like a cardboard barrel in one hand and a paper bag in the other. The tantalizing aroma was even stronger. She smiled and gestured with her head towards the dining alcove.

"Folks, dinner is served!" We sat at the table and hungrily watched Helen unpack a huge bucket of Kentucky Fried Chicken, fries, and coleslaw for dinner! There was Coke and 7UP – not in bottles but in the new pull-top cans like they had on TV! There were even paper plates, cups, straws, plastic cutlery, and paper napkins. I had never seen anything like it. Dinner delivered to the door – with plates! Wow!

My sister and I were wildly excited. We had seen the ads for KFC on TV but never imagined that we would eat it! Helen served us each some chicken, fries, and coleslaw. Giddy at the thought of having a second soft drink, I slowly reached for a Coke, expecting my mother to stop me. But nothing happened. What a treat! We had seconds and thirds and relished every greasy morsel until we felt sick and couldn't eat any more.

Mummy was quiet. She sat politely at the table. I didn't think she was enjoying herself. She gamely tried the chicken, coleslaw, and the fries but we could tell she didn't really like it.

"Who wants dessert?" said Helen, getting up from her chair. She emerged from the kitchen seconds later with her pièce de résistance – a store-bought, chocolate layer cake! It was big, gooey, and delicious, with bright green-and-blue flowers. Thick icing covered the entire cake. Just like the photos in the magazines! This was better than a Twinkie!

Helen asked my mother, "Coffee? I have decaf if you want."

"Certainly," replied Mummy with a polite, weary smile.

A few minutes later Helen brought my mother a mug of hot water. Then I watched, wide-eyed, as she opened a little orange envelope and stirred in a teaspoon of Sanka.

"Cream?" asked Helen, and when Mummy said yes, she passed her a brown glass jar. My mother looked at the jar, puzzled.

"It's Coffee-Mate – just put in a spoonful instead of coffee cream. The latest thing!" Helen explained, smiling.

"From the States, I suppose?" said Mummy, as Helen nodded her head.

The next evening, when Papa returned from his conference, I overheard Mummy telling him about our dinner at Helen's.

"Since when is ordering Kentucky Fried Chicken the same as having us over to dinner?" she exclaimed to my father who sat and listened.

"What is this Kentucky Fried Chicken, I don't think I've ever tasted it."

"An American chain restaurant. It's greasy and they cook the chicken with the skin on. But the girls were thrilled." My mother continued, "What galls me is that just last month we had them over for dinner – it was all home cooked. I slaved all day for them! Is this how they repay our hospitality?" The KFC dinner was joked about in our family for years.

Helen's daughter and I graduated from high school together and are still friends forty years later. Helen died a few years ago. Her daughter sent me an envelope full of clippings about her mother's professional life. Reading them, I suddenly realized that Helen was an accomplished academic whose husband's achievements had overshadowed hers. As I read about Helen's important work, I cringed at my only enduring memory of her – the KFC dinner. And then the penny dropped. Helen was an educated woman trying to carve out a career in the 1960s while raising three children. It had not occurred to me that she had neither the time nor the inclination to cook. When Helen invited our family to dinner, it wasn't about the food; she just wanted to see us. More than forty years later, I finally got it.

13

Urdu Made Easy

Mariam, Lahore, 1968

P apa scowls over the top of his glasses. He waves the blue
notebook at me.

*"Mariam, this homework is garbage. You can do better.
We'll try again tomorrow.*

*"You must learn some Urdu. It's part of your identity," he
says. Shaking his head and muttering under his breath, he
goes downstairs to watch Dick Cavett. I stand in the living
room, silently, hot tears slowly sliding down my cheeks.
Another Urdu lesson with my father ended badly.*

"Urdu? Never heard of it!" is what many people say when
they ask me what language is spoken in Pakistan. Even I was

surprised to learn that around three hundred million people speak Urdu, making it one of the world's most spoken tongues. This pales in comparison to my second language, French, only spoken by a mere seventy-six million.

Urdu is Pakistan's national language. Spoken, Urdu sounds very similar to Hindi (one of India's official languages) but it is written in a Persian script, whereas Hindi is written in the Sanskrit script. To my untrained ear, the two sound nearly identical. I reached this conclusion on the basis of many happy hours spent watching Bollywood movies and MTV India in Pakistani hotel rooms.

The *lingua franca* of my family household was English. My father told me that a specialist advised my parents that it would be difficult for me to deal with two languages at the same time so English prevailed. When I was an infant, my parents planned to settle permanently in Pakistan where I would have learned Urdu and Punjabi.

Things did not work out the way they had intended. Despite the dearth of qualified academics in early 1960s Pakistan, local universities had a perverse preference for foreign instructors. Prior to leaving for Canada in 1955, my father taught economics at Punjab University. He hoped to go back to Pakistan with his new PhD, Canadian wife, and daughter (me), but Papa was unsuccessful in negotiating his return. Disappointed, he decided to stay in Canada where he had better prospects. He pledged to take his children to Pakistan regularly and to teach us Urdu.

From age nine until eighteen, every weeknight, after dinner was finished and my school homework and chores were done, I joined my father in our living room for my Urdu lesson. Often, he conducted the lesson while reclined on the sofa, having just awoken from an after-dinner catnap. If the snooze went on longer because Papa was especially tired, then to my great relief, my Urdu lesson was cancelled. Other times, we would sit together at the dining room table and go over my homework.

A wise person once said that it is difficult to teach your own children. This certainly was the case with my father. He had high expectations of me. I, in turn, was not interested in learning the language of a country that didn't mean much to me. Growing up, I had never met another girl my own age that spoke Urdu. What use was a language when I didn't have anybody to speak it with? My grandfather and cousins in Pakistan spoke English, so what was the point of learning Urdu?

Sensing my lack of interest, my father tried to show me the bright side of learning Urdu.

"You know, Mariam, on the airplane we could speak Urdu to each other, and nobody would understand us. Like a secret language! Don't you think that would be great?"

I looked at my father and sank my awkward adolescent body further into my chair. He just didn't get it! I didn't want to be different. The thought of my father speaking to me in Urdu in public was mortifying. What if he did this in front of my friends? I wanted to fit in. Nobody I knew in Victoria spoke anything but English except the Chinese kids at school. But they were Chinese! Of course, they spoke Chinese! I was Canadian and I didn't want to speak a secret language. English was good enough for me and for everybody else around me in Victoria.

I was a good student, usually diligent about doing homework and always able to meet deadlines, but when it came to Urdu, I didn't make the effort. This attitude, in turn, deeply frustrated my father who linked success in my Urdu studies with sustaining the Pakistani-Canadian identity he wanted me to have. After all, how could I possibly have a meaningful connection to Pakistan when I didn't speak the language? I felt like a failure in Papa's eyes. Even though I insisted that I was Canadian and not Pakistani, I knew that I could have tried harder at Urdu. My frustrated father, tired at the end of a long day at the university, was an impatient and exacting teacher. He was determined; it cannot have been easy teaching Urdu to his sullen and uninterested daughter. Many an Urdu lesson ended with me in tears or my father shaking his head, his frustration and anger apparent. Yet we both persevered. Papa was unhappy with my progress, but he was always unfailingly supportive when his friends in Pakistan asked Papa why I didn't speak Urdu.

"Well, Mariam finds speaking Urdu challenging but she can read pretty well," my father would say. "Maybe someday she'll spend a few months in Pakistan and I'm sure she'll be fluent in no time."

It was a typical backhanded compliment from my father but still I was pleased.

Night after night, the teenage me trudged through Urdu *Dick and Jane*, totally bored by books designed for seven-year-olds. My father brought new Urdu books with him every time he went to Pakistan but the gap between the content of the books and my cultural reality as a Canadian teenager grew. Papa was determined to forge ahead but the lack of good teaching materials exacerbated his travails. In hindsight, he could have used fashion magazines or Bollywood movies to make the lessons more interesting or relatable for me. But this never would have occurred to my father, who was generally oblivious to popular culture.

On days when we were not at loggerheads over my pathetic efforts to do my Urdu homework he would say, "All you need is about six hundred words and you'll be fine. Just try a little harder. What if I'm delirious on my deathbed – how would you understand me?" This ominous threat made me cringe. I did not know what to say. For years, I was secretly haunted that I would not understand my father's last words. But when the end did come, he faded silently.

Over the years, I managed to pick up a few hundred words of vocabulary, some grammar, and the ability to read and write very basic Urdu. I suppose that, despite my attitude, some words penetrated my stubborn and unwilling adolescent brain. I can give directions to a Karachi taxi driver, make out roadside signs in rural Punjab, and tell an airport porter that I will not pay him more than ten rupees to carry my bag into the airport.

After I started university, the lessons became less frequent and finally stopped. I was surprised that I felt a void. I knew I had frittered away an opportunity. When I went on a trip to Pakistan with my father after the end of my first year at university, I felt self-conscious at my lack of fluency in Urdu. As I matured and came to terms with my cross-cultural background, I increasingly felt ashamed that I did not speak Urdu. Only as an adult did I realize the value of speaking another language.

For a long time, I convinced myself that I was utterly hopeless when it came to languages. This was easier than admitting that I hadn't tried or that my father had many talents but teaching Urdu was not one of them. I think that the fact that I was able to acquire a good level of fluency in French in my twenties partially compensated for my shaky grasp of Urdu and boosted my confidence. I had decided to stay in Montréal and knew that I needed to become relatively fluent in French in order to have a decent career.

When I moved to Montréal to study at McGill, I met, for the first time, people my own age who were from India and Pakistan. They spoke Urdu, Hindi, or other South Asian languages. No longer feeling like the only "Paki" in town, my attitude completely changed. I began to appreciate the value of knowing Urdu. Now that I was older, I embraced being different.

My Pakistani background and basic knowledge of the language helped me land my first job. After my first work trip to Pakistan as an adult, I resolved to improve my Urdu. This was not so easy, despite the fact that it is one of the world's most spoken languages. It is difficult to find Urdu courses – Italian, Portuguese, Russian, and even Korean were regularly offered in Montréal's adult education centres but never Urdu.

As I pursued my career in international development, often working in Pakistan, I discovered that I understood much more than I realized. On my first visit to a village, my Pakistani interpreter looked at me, amused, when she realized that I was taking many of my notes without waiting for translation. We interviewed women about their work in the fields and I knew the names of all the crops and vegetables grown in Pakistan. It seems that some words stuck in my brain despite my stubbornness. Decades later, I regret never having learned to read Urdu well.

مریم

Papa's letters to his father and brothers were in a box in the back of one of his closets. Found after his death, written in faded fountain pen ink on thin blue aerogrammes or onionskin paper, they bore postmarks from London and later from Canada in the 1950s, '60s, and '70s. As I held a packet of letters bound together with a brittle rubber band, I remembered my father talking about them when I was a teen. Unable to be in Lahore for *Dada Abajee's* funeral, Papa visited several months later. When he came home and opened his suitcase, it was full of big brown envelopes containing letters my father and my mother had written to their father and father-in-law over the years. In particular, I remembered Papa talking about one letter that he found.

"I came across a letter that I assumed had been lost in the mail. There it was, neatly slit open with a knife," said Papa. "An acceptance letter to the PhD programme in economics at Harvard University. You see, at *Dada Abajee's* house, mail arrived twice a day. It would be brought to my father for distribution to my brothers and me. My father didn't want me to go to the USA and by withholding the letter he made sure that I didn't go there to study," Papa sighed.

"For years, I wondered why I never heard back from Harvard. I had been selected as a student scholar in their

International Summer Programme – I think it was in the summer of 1953. Goddammit, I even had a reference letter from Henry Kissinger! But my father wanted me to stay within the Commonwealth. He didn't like the US, so that sealed my fate," Papa said, shrugging his shoulders. "I'll never know what my life would have been like had I got the Harvard letter." I looked at my father, stunned, trying to imagine how he felt.

Decades later, I reached into the box. The bulk of the correspondence was between Papa and his father, my *Dada Abajee*, but there were letters written to Middle Uncle or Big Uncle. I picked up one letter and then another – most of them were written in Urdu, the language my father used for correspondence with his family. But there was also a stack of letters from my mother to her father-in-law in Pakistan – all in English.

Just three years after his life was completely uprooted by the tragedy of Partition, Papa sailed to England, via the Suez Canal, to study in London. This was where the letters began.

My eyes lingered over a few English words sprinkled throughout the letters. One, dated July 1955, was written while my father was on a boat in the Suez Canal, yet another on a transatlantic crossing from England to Canada. I picked up the letters and scrutinized them more closely. While my mother's handwriting was always relatively small and thus familiar, my father wrote in English in a large, expansive hand. But when he wrote in Urdu, his writing was much smaller, and it was strange to see what I knew was his handwriting and yet not recognize it as my own father's. Did he write so small because he was trying to fit as much as possible into one aerogramme?

I recognized some of the return addresses. Papa's first address in Montréal is now the site of a commercial building. Another address is on a downtown street that has changed names since he lived there.

As I gazed at the sea of letters, I felt helpless. I knew that I should have been able to read them. The fact that I couldn't made me angry. I wondered how I could have been so stupid.

How I wished I had all the time in the world! I could sit down with a few dictionaries, struggle through the letters, and gradually teach myself how to read Urdu. I imagine it would take me a couple of years to get to the level that I would need to be at in order to understand these letters. But the luxury of time eludes me and so I have relied on friends and a couple of Pakistani students studying at McGill.

Papa's letters home were full of witty and sarcastic observations. Marukh, a Pakistani student, laughed as she translated my father's letter written while passing through the Suez Canal. Papa did not hold back when commenting on his fellow Pakistanis traveling on the same ship; in particular, he took umbrage at their strong body odour and poor table manners. He noted that his countrymen had yet to discover modern inventions such as deodorant!

For the most part I was struck by the banality of the letters between Papa and his father. They wrote to each other in a highly formal and archaic form of Urdu that is rarely used today. This came as no surprise. My strongest memories of my grandfather were of a distant and somewhat cold man. Back and forth the letters go. They wrote of the weather, Papa enclosing the occasional newspaper article about record low temperatures. Then there were money transfers, my father's regular requests for books and other research material needed for his PhD thesis, and his future employment prospects. My grandfather, *Dada Abajee*, constantly asked his son when he would finish his studies because he wanted him home.

The letters also gave me considerable insight into their relationship. When I was both a teenager and a young woman, my father constantly held himself up as a paragon of virtue when it came to dealing with his father. According to Papa, he was always honest, forthright, and truthful with his father. His letters told me otherwise. In fact, my father reveals little of his life in Canada that is really meaningful. He never talks of friends, of girlfriends, and in fact wrote a letter to his father three weeks after he and my mother were married in which he confesses that he is thinking of marrying a Canadian woman!

Then there is a gap in the correspondence. The obvious conclusion is that my father censored his letters to *Dada Abajee* because both men were far too meticulous to have lost or misplaced several months' worth of letters. Papa only wanted us to know so much. He knew that my Urdu-speaking friends could be called upon to help and make up for my lack of fluency.

Papa understood the value of speaking more than one language and he prized his linguistic heritage. My father knew five languages but lived most of his life in the last language he learned – English. He mastered English, loved London, but never forgot the British had colonized his country. Papa was especially proud of his proficiency in South Asian languages, particularly Urdu, which has a rich literary tradition. One of my favourite stories about my father illustrates this.

After retiring, Papa moved back to Québec from British Columbia. As is possible between Canadian provinces, he wished to transfer his driver's license. He went to the appropriate office of the Government of Québec, took a number, and waited. Although the official language of the Government of Québec is French, certain services are offered in English. Transfer of a driver's license was one of the few bilingual services available at the time. A few minutes later, when his number was called, he went to the counter and started to speak in English.

The francophone clerk rolled her eyes and muttered, "Mon dieu! Un autre anglais qui ne parle pas français." (Oh my God! It's another one of those English people who don't speak a word of French.) She scowled over the counter at my father. Papa slid his glasses halfway down his nose and looked the clerk straight in the eye. He flashed a charming smile at her and started to speak.

"My dear lady, English is not my first language. I am not English. You are insulting me by calling me this name. I learned Punjabi, Kashmiri, Arabic, and Urdu before I even knew a word of English. That's a total of five languages – English was the last one I learned. The British didn't just colonize Québec – they colonized India too. And we kicked them out of our country. My dear lady, you need to read some history."

The clerk looked at him in stunned silence.

Gleefully telling the story to me the next day, he said, "After that, the pipsqueak clerk shut up and spoke to me in English."

After I started to write this chapter, I pulled a battered blue folder off my bookshelf. The handwritten and yellowed label was marked "Urdu Books." A couple of big fat elastics were wrapped around the folder to keep it closed. I removed them and opened the folder. Inside was a pile of old workbooks and textbooks. One, *Urdu Made Easy*, caught my eye. The full title of the book was *Urdu Made Easy: Being an Easy Guide to Conversation Adapted for the Use of Foreigners* by the late Prof. Aziz-ur-Rahman. My copy was the fifty-fourth printing, dated July 1969. The first was in September 1915, a century ago. I flipped through the book – it didn't look too difficult, especially since all of the Urdu vocabulary was written in English script.

The blue folder also contained ten notebooks of Urdu homework from 1967 to 1977. My father assigned me translations, lists of vocabulary, and even dictations. As I shuffled through my notes, I felt a tinge of regret and shame as I realized the effort and time Papa had put into planning our lessons. But I was also impressed to see just how much work I had put into my Urdu classes – page after page of neat writing in English in a childlike shaky Urdu script. I had done a lot. Why was I so hard on myself? Or was I reflecting my father's high standard? Sadly, after so many years of study, I was unable to converse in Urdu.

The folder of Urdu notebooks and textbooks has always been on my bookshelf. It was packed up by movers and accompanied me to Africa and Asia and back to Montréal.

I showed this folder to my husband. "Look at all I did!" I said, leafing through the yellowed pages and colourful Urdu ABCs.

My husband asked me why I kept this battered file for so many years. I told him I wasn't sure why, that I had to think about it. The next day I realized what it was – I held onto that blue folder with the same determination that my father showed by persisting with my Urdu lessons for all those years. Urdu classes were an important part of my childhood and adolescence. Throwing the folder away meant closing the door forever on the possibility that I would become fluent in Papa's language. Unlike the title of the book, for me, Urdu had never been easy. But it's not impossible.

14

Sunday School for Muslims

Papa, Edmonton Mosque, 1981

"But Papa, what is a sta-lis-ti-cal Muslim? Is it like a fraction? I don't understand ... You never let me do anything fun." On the brink of tears, I sniffed loudly.

Papa leaned back in his big office chair in his basement study. He put down his *Pakistan Times* newspaper, looked me straight in the eye, and said, "All right, Mariam. I'll think about what you've said. And stop crying. Here's a tissue. And it's Sta-TIS-tical, not sta-LIS-tical."

I was twelve years old and straining for more independence. Papa had just denied me permission for yet another activity, invoking vague religious reasons for not allowing me to go to Nancy's slumber party.

"But why can't I go? Where does it say that Muslims can't go to slumber parties? It's going to be all girls anyways."

Papa crossed his arms and looked at me. "Well, Mariam, what would you do if breakfast the next morning is bacon and eggs? Would you eat it?"

Papa's question startled me. I didn't know what to say so I stared at the floor while clenching a wad of humid tissues.

He scowled. "Just as I thought, you would have eaten it rather than say no. You're ashamed and embarrassed by your Muslim identity. I know that you want to be like everyone else, but I'm afraid you never will be."

I didn't reply. My father was right. I wouldn't have refused the hypothetical bacon. I hated being different.

Papa was always talking about my Muslim identity. I didn't really understand what he meant. It was like a floating balloon that was always just out of reach. Being Muslim was a big drag. There wasn't anything good about it. Muslim meant that I was never allowed to have any fun – like going to slumber parties and school dances.

I asked my father what a Muslim was. His reply was that we were "statistical Muslims." I had no idea what he was talking about, being several years away from studying statistics. I knew being Muslim had something to do with Papa being from Pakistan. But Pakistan had been just great! My Pakistan, at least my last visit when I was ten, had been a whirling free-for-all. Everybody in Pakistan was a Muslim and I had a terrific time there! So why did being Muslim in Canada mean I could never have any fun? I just didn't get it.

I wanted to be like everybody else. It was simple – if bacon and eggs had been served at a friend's house, I would have eaten them. I was just a typical 1970s teenager. I wanted to fit in, be popular, and maybe, if I was lucky, get a boyfriend. My head was filled with fantasies of that cute guy in grade ten asking me to the dance or dreaming that I had returned to school after the Christmas holidays wearing fabulous new clothes that had been waiting for me under the perfectly decorated tree.

My parents were not particularly religious. Now, decades later, I finally see that was actually the root of the problem. It's difficult for parents who have turned their backs on their religious upbringing to then inculcate their children with the same dogma that they rejected.

My mother grew up in a Polish Catholic family in Chapleau, Ontario where she attended church, had her communion, and grew increasingly skeptical about Catholicism, especially as it applied to women. By the time she was in her late teens she moved to Toronto. One of her first acts of defiance was to stop going to church. To the best of my knowledge, she only stepped inside a church once again in her life. A friend she made in one of her university courses, Mary, was a regular churchgoer and a practising Catholic. It took Mary several years, but she finally convinced my mother to go to church with her one day.

"I couldn't believe the difference!" said Mummy when she came home. "There was no more Latin mass." I looked at her, puzzled, which caused her to go into an explanation of Vatican II, and what mass was like when she was a child.

"It was like a performance, going to church. Maybe that's where I got my love of the theatre," she speculated.

"Are you going to go back to church?" I asked. "Do you like it?"

"Oh no, dear girl. I couldn't go back regularly. I just don't believe all that stuff anymore. It was nice to see how things have changed. And that's enough for me."

Islam does not require non-Muslims who marry Muslims to convert. My mother remained a lapsed Catholic all of her life. She was knowledgeable about Islam; tutored by my father and as a result of her own reading and research. In particular, she used to read books by Muslim feminists and was particularly critical of the whole system known as *purdah*, by which men and women lived almost entirely separate lives. It was my mother who explained to me, prior to my first visit to Pakistan as a young woman, that men who would appear to ignore me were actually being polite. She also educated me about not shaking hands with unrelated men and to not expect gestures of warmth and affection from my male relatives.

My father attended a mosque school across the street from his family home until he was ten. My grandfather was a very religious man who prayed five times a day for his entire life. Yet Papa was quick to emphasize that he did not grow up in an intolerant or strictly religious environment.

"My father's legal practice included clients from all religious groups, and I remember him going to Hindu and other religious celebrations, invited by his clients. Back then, the narrow and intolerant brand of Islam that is so prevalent now was restricted to a tiny group of illiterate Saudi goat herders."

When he was twenty-five years old, my father sailed from Pakistan to London where he attended graduate school. I believe that in London he gradually shrugged off some of the rules that he had grown up with. Papa learned to love British beer. He ate meat that wasn't *halal* and tried the forbidden bacon. But once he had children, pork was definitely taboo. He would never admit to having tried bacon in London; it was one of his old friends from graduate school who told me about this. Papa always denied the story.

I started to realize that I was different once I started school. My life did not include church on Sundays or Sunday school. When I started grade one, I had never heard of the Lord's Prayer nor did I know to bend my head down when reciting it, but I quickly caught on by looking at the other kids around me.

I cannot remember exactly how old I was when I realized that I was a Muslim. But as a young girl, whenever I was denied permission to do something, if my father was involved in the decision, the fact that I was a Muslim was often trotted out as the reason. By my early teens, I challenged my father's rules and restrictions more and more. I asked how and why being a Muslim meant that I could not do many of the things I wanted to do. I really didn't understand what being Muslim was except as a negative factor invoked by my father to deny me all sorts of activities.

"But Papa," I'd say, "how am I supposed to learn what a Muslim is? Mummy can't teach me. All I learn about at school is Christianity. How can you expect me to be a Muslim when I don't really know what it's all about?"

I'm sure my parents discussed the religious identity of their children well before my sister and I were even born. Then, like all parents, they just got busy. My father was establishing his career as an academic in a new university and was also involved in university politics and administration. Much of the daily business of child rearing was left to my mother. My cry for help with my religious identity woke my father up to the reality that he could not expect my mother to give his children the tools they needed to be Muslims, statistical or otherwise.

Victoria in the 1960s and '70s was a very white, Christian town. Most people were of British origin but there were also Norwegians, Germans, and Dutch. A sprinkling of Sikhs, a tiny Chinatown, and the odd Japanese-Canadian who had survived internment during World War II called Victoria home. There were a few Afro-Americans – draft dodgers and university professors. Several Jewish families.

Double-decker London buses with huge Union Jacks painted on their sides plied tourists around a city that sold itself as being a bit of jolly olde England in Canada. Most of the kids I went through elementary and high school with were of English, Scottish, or Northern European backgrounds. The exceptions were one Aboriginal girl, a Hawaiian, a handful of Chinese kids, an Afro-American or two, and a South Asian girl whose family had been kicked out of Idi Amin's Uganda.

When I was in grade four, my father took a sabbatical and we moved back to Montréal for one year. I spent the last six weeks of the school year at Roslyn School in Westmount, Montréal's English enclave. I completed grade five at the same school. It was the happiest year of my childhood. I had fantastic teachers, nobody struggled with my name the way they did in Victoria, and there were other kids who weren't Christian. When I went with my father to Pakistan in December 1968, nobody thought it was strange. One kid in my class remembered visiting the Pakistani pavilion at Expo 67! There were Jewish kids in my class who took days off from school for Jewish holidays. One of them, Merle, took Hebrew lessons after school. I took a big risk and confided in her about my Urdu lessons with my father. It was the first time I had ever mentioned these lessons to one of my friends from school. She told her Hebrew teacher about me. Merle's Hebrew teacher showed her the similarities between the Arabic and Hebrew alphabets. I can still remember that she explained to me how similar some of the letters were. I thrived in this environment but after a year in cosmopolitan Montréal, it was back to Victoria.

The main difference that I remember upon returning to Victoria after a year in Montréal was that there were two new shopping centres and a McDonald's restaurant. But Victoria did not escape Canada's growing multiculturalism. As the swinging sixties faded, Canada was more ethnically diverse. This change was barely noticeable in Victoria, but if you looked closely, there were some small signs. By the early 1970s, the family who had escaped Idi Amin started Victoria's first Indian restaurant. Another mixed couple – he was Indian, and she was English – moved into our neighbourhood. Ron, the son of a very British couple on Alpine Crescent, married a Chinese-Canadian woman.

Victoria's South Asian community mostly consisted of Sikhs who had come to Vancouver Island to work in the lumber industry. My father tried to meet any Pakistanis and fellow Muslims, no matter where they were from, who lived in Victoria. They would be invited to the house for a meal and to meet the family. An elderly couple from Iran came to dinner one night. The talk turned to languages and then all of a sudden, my father was reading out loud from a Persian book! I had no idea that he knew some Persian – the couple complimented him on his accent and later he told me he had studied Persian as a young boy in school.

When I was a teenager, our family attended an *Eid* celebration in Victoria. It was an attempt by my father to socialize with the small but growing Pakistani Muslim community. The four of us descended rickety stairs into a brightly lit church basement. The scene was chaotic and loud: Pakistani music blared from tinny speakers, screaming kids ran around like maniacs, and a teenage girl with an early version of a video camera stuck a big microphone in my face telling me to, "Say something!"

I, of course, was absolutely tongue-tied. My parents were the only mixed couple, and the room was separated into men's and women's zones. Most of the women were illiterate and did not speak much English. Not speaking more than a few words of Urdu or Punjabi, my mother could only sit there and watch the melee. My university professor father did not fare much better, as he found himself in the middle of a group of rural Punjabis with whom he had little in common since he was highly educated and from the big city of Lahore.

In Pakistan, huge cleavages, economic, cultural, and linguistic, exist between urban and rural areas. Even though they were all in Canada, and all Muslims, the differences persisted. We never went to one of those events again, my father preferring to celebrate *Eid* at home.

My father tried his best to show his children the Canadian face of Islam, even trekking to Edmonton to show us what was the only mosque in western Canada. Once there, I don't recall if he went inside or even if he prayed. It was important that my father showed us the building as a symbol of the Muslim presence in Canada.

For Papa, religion was private. He felt comfortable with his identity and didn't have to prove his faith. He hated outward displays of religiosity and did not want any version of Islam imposed upon him. After Pakistan International Airlines banned alcohol on its international flights, he never flew them again except to travel within Pakistan where he had no choice.

Once I flew with him between Karachi and Lahore. When a prayer before travel drifted out over the public address system in the airplane, Papa rolled his eyes and muttered something about the piety of the airline managers! He was disgusted by the public banning of consumption of alcohol because of the hypocrisy it created. He even let his Pakistani passport lapse because he refused to sign a declaration that he was a Muslim. "It's none of their bloody business," he said.

My father had what I now realize was a very Western interpretation of Islam in that it was individualistic, rather than being based on adherence and conformity to the wider expectations of a group or society.

Never once in my life did I see Papa wearing the male version of the *shalwar kameez*. Muslim men in Pakistan wear this garment when they go to pray at the mosque on Fridays. I cannot recall my father ever going to Friday prayers. He always said he found Western clothing more comfortable. The only exception was the typical Punjabi ankle-length loincloth, or *lunghi*, that he used to wear around the house.

There were subtle signs of my father's Muslim identity. He treated his copy of the Koran that had been given to him by his father when he left for Canada with respect and taught me to do the same. On one of his trips back to Lahore he brought his old prayer mat back with him. He hung it on the wall of his study in a place where he saw it every day. I think it was important to him to see this symbol.

A few days after our conversation about the slumber party, Papa announced that he was starting his own Sunday school and that I was to be the only pupil. My religious lessons took place on Sundays, after the family had eaten brunch and listened to the Sunday morning news show on the radio. Papa prepared lessons and assignments for me, which I completed. I still have my notebooks from these lessons – I keep them in the same battered blue file folder where I have all my Urdu exercises.

Flipping through the pages, I stop at one dated January 9, 1977. I was halfway through my first year of university. In addition, I still had the occasional religious lesson. My homework was to write definitions of the major sects in Islam. Papa also assigned me an essay on the life of the Prophet Muhammad. I still have it, written by hand on lined paper. On the first page my father wrote: "A for a very good effort and a well-written essay. Papa."

My father also made me photocopies from a prayer book showing the various positions for prayer. He even recorded a cassette tape of prayers for me. It is probably the only recording I have of my father's voice. I don't even have a cassette player on which to play it. A label on the cassette tape itself says in my father's meticulous way, "Prayer for Mariam," and is dated August 1983. At the time, I had just started to work on my MA thesis. Like some of my Urdu exercises that I dragged around the world for decades, I cannot bear to part with these tattered notebooks and old tapes.

The religious lessons went better than my fraught Urdu lessons. They were in English and easier for my social scientist father to teach. Papa had a comprehensive knowledge of Islam. It was only when I was older that I realized that his interpretation was unique in its modern liberal perspective. Many years later, after he retired, he published two books on Islam, thus putting his extensive expertise to good use. Papa's interpretation of the Koran made me think. For example, he regularly reminded me that Islam was a very young religion, equivalent to Christianity 1300 years ago.

His appreciation for European history, acquired when he was a PhD student teaching an economic history course, astonished me. Papa explained that in Christian terms, Islam was actually a medieval religion that was being dragged into the twentieth century. He lamented the demise of early Muslim society, which had emphasized learning and women's education. My father often put Islamic practices in a historical context. So, while he viewed the tradition of giving women half the inheritance of men to be grossly unequal, he would say, "At the time that the Koran was written, the desert societies where Muhammed lived did not give any inheritance rights whatsoever to women. So you see, Mariam, it was an improvement."

On the practice of polygamy, my father pointed out that the declaration allowing it was made during a time when there were many wars in Arabia, which had resulted in a large population of young widows.

"But if you read the Koran carefully," said Papa, "It is clear that a man should treat all of his wives equally. And that is practically impossible. So, in reality, polygamy was only sanctioned under very specific circumstances."

He continued. "Same thing with alcohol. Even today, some Arabs drink a wine made from fermented dates – although they don't want to admit it. The Koran has the same warnings as any other religious text, which is not to drink excessively. It's all a question of interpretation."

Papa wagged his index finger at me and said, "Did you know that Indonesian Muslims eat a type of wild boar that is a member of the swine family? It's one of their sole sources of animal protein. See how flexible Islam can be?"

"And speaking about pork, the whole reason that Muslims, Jews, and most Christians in the Middle East don't eat pork is because it was susceptible to disease at a time when there was no refrigeration. Holy books like the Koran and the Torah prescribed ways of life for their followers, including guidance on what foods were safe to eat."

My father had no use for conservative Islam. In his opinion, its adherents practiced perversions of what he viewed to be a very open and inclusive religion. Around the time that my religious lessons began, OPEC I and II had led to the creation of great wealth in Saudi Arabia and other conservative Gulf states. Papa was disgusted with all the money that they "donated" to poor countries like Pakistan to spread their conservative brand of Islam. "It's only going to end badly," he predicted. Looking back, he was prescient indeed.

Symbols and rituals were very important for Papa. I never saw him fast for *Ramadan*, but he liked to make a special meal to mark *Eid*, the end of a month of fasting. As a teenager, I criticized these dinners, declaring them devoid of meaning because I had no childhood memories to connect them to. I used to tell my father that I didn't think I deserved *Eid* dinner because I hadn't fasted for the month – and for that matter, he hadn't fasted either. He disagreed, arguing that the act of celebrating was significant, and pointed out that there were many Christians who made a turkey at Christmas simply because they loved to eat it and enjoyed the tradition.

Since my father died, I make my own *Eid* dinners as a way of paying him tribute. I comb through my collection of family recipes, selecting the ones that I will prepare. I grind the spices and cook an array of dishes, which I think my father would have enjoyed. I can almost hear him looking up from his plate with a smile and saying, "Very tasty, Mariam."

My father always said that one of the things he valued about Islam was that there was no structured church or clergy. "Nobody can tell you that you are a Muslim because all you have to say is that you are a Muslim and that is it. The rest is between you and God." He would chuckle and point at the sky. To use the current parlance, I self-identify as a Muslim. I don't call myself a statistical Muslim, although now I understand what my father meant.

Most Canadians do not connect me to Pakistan or see even the slightest hint in my demeanor or appearance that jives with their perception of what a Muslim woman looks like. My husband enjoys provoking people by slipping slyly into the conversation that he married a Muslim.

مریم

We are attending a friend's birthday party at a chic Italian restaurant.

"You don't look like a Pakistani," says the man whose wife just introduced us.

"I'm not. I'm Canadian," I reply patiently with a smile.

"But you were born there, right?"

"Nope, I was born at the Royal Victoria Hospital," I say, referring to one of Montréal's major medical centres.

The husband persists. "But the colour of your skin – please don't take this the wrong way – but is your father dark?"

"Well, I wouldn't say he was dark, but I'm lighter than him. My mother was Polish-Canadian. And did you know that there are people in Pakistan with blue or green eyes? Some are descendants of Alexander the Great's army."

"Okay, I get it. But you don't look like a Muslim. Where is your head covering? Isn't that mandatory?" Hubby looks very perplexed.

This conversation is typical of the interactions I've had with people for most of my adult life. When I tell them that I'm a Muslim, my physical appearance as a modern secular woman in typical Canadian clothing with no head covering contradicts their images of Muslim women shrouded in a hijab, a niqab, or some such garment. I like to think that I'm educating people that Islam is more than crazy people on TV yelling "Allah ho Akbar" or shapeless women draped in yards of black fabric.

I learned my lessons well at Papa's Sunday school for Muslims. In discussions with friends and acquaintances, I enjoy flinging out an unusual fact or two that my father taught me, such as the rationales behind polygamy and female inheritance. I have picked up a few zingers of my own over the years, such as the fact that Muslims copied Jewish kosher rituals and even recite the same prayer, translated into Arabic from Hebrew, when slaughtering animals. This is a good anecdote to tell religious Muslims or Jews. I remind all who will listen that Ataturk outlawed the veil in Turkey, that only wealthy Muslim women have the luxury of covering their faces, and that one would search high and low for a female veiled face harvesting rice in rural Pakistan. I especially enjoy sharing my observation that there is a considerable resemblance between the *hijab* and the habit that Catholic nuns used to wear until just fifty years ago! Once the analogy sinks in, many people agree with me.

Eventually, I studied statistics and I understood the nuance of my father's self-identification as a statistical Muslim. I never really felt comfortable with it. It's too academic and dry a characterization. As far as I am concerned, my identity is more than just a number; it is an integral part of who I am. My Islam is secular, and my sense of identity is extremely strong. I still do not eat pork although I have cheated a few times in my life and admit to this freely. I think that my father's efforts to give me a Muslim identity were successful; I am not particularly religious, yet I strongly identify with the broad teachings of Islam. I will never know for sure, but I suspect that's what Papa was trying to achieve.

I married Eli – he is Jewish. As my parents had done, we were married in a civil ceremony presided over by a Unitarian church celebrant. My husband says that he became more Jewish when he married me. I would say the same thing about my Muslim identity.

Our relationship is tolerant and based on mutual respect and understanding. In our house we celebrate everything – our annual flagship dinners, as I call them, are for Passover, *Eid*, Thanksgiving, and Christmas. I have even engaged in some religious cross-fertilization, borrowing the Passover tradition of reading the Passover story for our *Eid* celebration, where we tell the *Eid* saga. The family and friends seated around our holiday tables reflect the diversity of our lives and beliefs from atheism to Buddhism and beyond. Each December we hold two parties – one for Christmas, the other for Hanukkah. Throughout the month, a silver tinsel tree with a Star of David on the top glistens in the corner. I'm still trying to find a combination crescent and Star of David ornament.

I know my father fretted endlessly that I would lose my identity if I married somebody who was not a fellow statistical Muslim. But this has not happened. Instead, I revel in my multicultural and multifaith life.

Eli and I do not eat pork or keep any pork products in the house. But we're both rather fond of turkey bacon so we don't feel deprived. While both Muslims and Jews share the pork taboo, my exposure to Eli's family has shown me a wide range of interpretations of keeping kosher.

When discussing my religious identity with new friends and acquaintances, I'm often asked what sect I'm from. I suspect it's because whomever I'm talking to is having a hard time connecting me to what they see as a repressive and medieval religion. There are days that I talk to them about the sophisticated and highly educated women I know in Pakistan who do not cover their heads, who are articulate and outspoken, and who know how to drive a car. Other times, I'm not really in the mood to have that discussion, so I flippantly say that I'm from a martini-drinking sect of Islam. I explain that my father really enjoyed a dry martini at the end of the day. That always gets me a laugh. Perhaps Papa is up there in heaven, sipping on a martini and watching over my shoulder as I type these words. And if he is – well, Papa, here's to Sunday school for Muslims. You did a wonderful

job of teaching me about Islam and I am eternally grateful.
I'll drink to that.

15

The Boyfriend Club (I)

Mariam, 1975

When I got to my locker at lunchtime Monday, Alasdair was leaning against it, a cocky smile on his freckled face.

"What's up, Alasdair?"

"Well, after the dance on Friday, I assume that we're going around now. Correct?" I smiled back but didn't answer.

Me, Mariam Pal, going around with Alasdair? Does this mean I have a boyfriend now?

"Want to eat lunch together?"

"Sure, sounds good," I said as I trailed my new boyfriend down the hall. We ate lunch together every day that week. After lunch we'd walk to the corner store, holding hands, and Alasdair bought me a fudgesicle, even though it was December.

Alasdair had freckles, was cute, witty, and he was in grade twelve. I was in grade eleven. He'd brought a micro-minied Janet Riverton to the dance three days earlier. Boys noticed Janet. Long midis may have been in, but Janet showed off her long legs in teensy-weensy skirts and sheer beige nylons. I was still in leotards and knee socks; my mother refused to buy me stockings because I ran them within five minutes. Next to Janet I looked like a five-year-old. With glasses.

But Alasdair had spent the evening with me!!

On Tuesday, Alasdair asked me to go out with him that weekend. My first date! But I needed my Pakistani father's permission. I decided to speak to him that evening before dinner.

From the time I was thirteen, my father's Pakistani universe and my Canadian teenage world collided with increasing frequency. Asking Papa if I could go on my first date was, in my sixteen-year-old world, the biggest challenge I had ever faced. I was petrified he would say no. The prospect was simply too gruesome to even contemplate. I took a deep breath and started to speak.

"Papa." My voice was hoarse. I perched on the edge of the big kitchen chair, the one where my father always sat. The chair was bigger than the others – it was also the most comfortable. My sister and I both fought to sit in it. Tonight,

I had got there first. The chair gave me confidence yet somehow, I felt so small. "I have something to ask you." My voice faded. I clenched my hands so tightly they hurt. I could feel my nails digging into my palms as a drop of sweat started to slowly descend down my torso.

"Yes," said Papa, not really paying attention. He was busy discussing the day with my mother as she made dinner. Standing in a corner of the kitchen, he sipped his nightly cocktail from a happy face glass. Papa leaned back against the kitchen counter, bracing himself with one arm. With the other arm he swirled his drink in the glass. I could hear the ice cubes clinking.

"What is it?" he said, as he took a sip.

The words tore out of my mouth: "I-have-a-boyfriend-his-name-is-Alasdair-please-can-I-go-out-with-him-on-Friday?" Underarms drenched in sweat, I gripped my arms tightly across my chest. My mother opened the oven door, and I could smell the sizzling meatloaf. I felt sick to my stomach as tears started to roll down my cheeks. I knew what was coming.

"No! No daughter of mine will date boys. You are a Pakistani, a Muslim girl, and cannot date. You must concentrate on your studies. Your math is poor. Then you will go to university."

"No!" I cried out. "You're always trying to control me. I live in a prison camp, not a house. He's my boyfriend. You can't stop me." Reaching towards the table I grabbed a fistful of tissues. I took off my glasses and blotted my eyes. "How can you do this to me? I'm Canadian, not Pakistani! I was born here. And I'm a good student; if it weren't for math, I'd have made the honour roll."

"I see. A Ca-NA-di-an girl? Well, my dear girl, you don't look like a nice, white, Christian Ca-NA-di-an. Maybe you should change your name to Debbie. Or Marilyn." Papa sipped his martini and scowled.

"If you didn't want me to grow up in Canada then why did you come here?" I dabbed my eyes with tissue. "You never let me do anything. All I do is stay at home. I'm sixteen years old!! I'm not a child!!"

I was too young to realize that the worst time to approach Papa was while he martinied down from another day of genteel racism. One of a handful of non-white professors at the university, my father suffered discreet discrimination for years. It must have been excruciating for a man who had graduated at the top of his class at the London School of Economics. Canada had let him down. Now his daughter had turned into a Canadian teenager.

Papa put his drink down, cleared his throat and looked at me. "Mariam, my position is clear. You will not date. Since you started high school four years ago, I have allowed you to attend school dances even though this type of socializing is not part of my culture. I have compromised enough. You can cry and shout all you want but I will not change my mind." He looked at me with all the confidence of an autocrat as he finished his martini. I had been dismissed.

"No, no, no," I wailed. "If you don't let me go then the whole school will be laughing at me. And it will all be your fault. Oh, God! I wish I were dead." Sobbing, I stumbled down the hall to my bedroom. I slammed the door and threw myself onto my bed face down, burying my head in the pillow. I had floated on air since Friday's dance but now I felt like crawling into bed and never coming out.

For years, no boy I liked had ever noticed me. And now that I had finally found a boyfriend, my father wouldn't let me go out. It was all so unfair.

Curled on my bed in the fetal position my mind returned to Friday's dance. A few minutes after my mother dropped me off at the school entrance, I stood on the edge of the dance floor with my friend, Laurie. The band played the opening chords to "Jumping Jack Flash." Alasdair bounded out of nowhere, grabbed my hand, and pulled me onto the dance floor. We danced to every song until the band took a break, right after a slow dance to Joe Cocker's "You are so Beautiful." Locked in an awkward but satisfying embrace, I felt Alasdair's face so close to mine that his breath fogged up my glasses. Sitting in a stairwell, we cooled down over our 7UPs. We talked. Alasdair wanted to be a journalist. When I told him I wanted to be a lawyer he started to laugh. I was mad and started to walk away. I don't remember why I stayed or what Alasdair said to make me change my mind. After the break we danced nonstop until the last song of the night – "Stairway to Heaven." I melted into Alasdair's arms.

On Monday, the whole school was talking about how Alasdair dumped Janet for "Mariam the brain" at the dance. Although I was not proud of stealing another girl's date, I enjoyed feeling like a femme fatale in one of those Bette Davis movies that I used to watch on PBS with my mother. Finally, a cute, smart boy liked me! He even told me my glasses were "pretty spacey." I was giddy with happiness.

And now, what if my father said no? Would I ever join the boyfriend club?

مريم

My parents' voices drifted down the hallway under my bedroom door. "They date at sixteen now. Frances and I were discussing all this just last week. It's only a date – it's not as if she's going to marry him," said my mother. Then my father: "It starts with a date – next thing you know she'll be at church every Sunday." Their voices faded as I bawled over the certain death of my dream of belonging to the boyfriend club.

Click. My bedroom door opened. It was my mother.

"Let me talk to your father. He's had a long day. Remember what happened about the dances."

I sniffled and said, "Okay."

When I started high school, my father refused to allow me to go to any of the school dances. I desperately wanted to go. It was always the same reason – I was Muslim and Pakistani. Eventually, with the support of my Canadian mother, Papa relented, and I was allowed to attend three out of four dances per year. My father never explained, nor did I ask, why he made me skip one of the dances. Would he capitulate and let me go out with my boyfriend?

Wednesday. Thursday. The wait was excruciating. I overheard snippets of my parents talking in the middle of the night and whispered telephone updates to my friend Laurie. When I was not at school I moped around the house, avoiding my father. I did extra math exercises sitting at the dining room table so my parents could see how diligent I was.

On Thursday evening, about an hour after dinner, my mother came to my room. "So, what are you going to wear tomorrow night?" she asked me with a weary smile. Papa had said yes! I was ecstatic.

Friday night. The doorbell rang. I sprinted down the stairs and opened the door to a grinning Alasdair.

"Hi, Alasdair! Come in and meet my parents."

Alasdair wore a shirt that was half unbuttoned down his hairless chest and a green checked sports jacket. He had a wisp of a mustache.

"Aren't you going to be cold, dressed so lightly in December?" asked my father.

"Oh, no sir. I'll be fine."

Alasdair helped me put on my winter coat and we sauntered out the door. Holding hands, we walked to the bus stop. I wished it were daytime so the whole neighbourhood could see us. At last, I had joined the boyfriend club.

مریم

O n the last day of school before the Christmas holidays, Alasdair gave me a small package.

"Open it." I looked inside and saw a silver ring. "It's the one you admired at the Christmas Craft Fair," said Alasdair.

"It's so romantic!" gushed Laurie when I showed it to her.

"A ring? After only two weeks? Give it back," snapped my mother in the kitchen when I came home from school.

"I'm not giving it back. It was a gift. Why do you have to make such a big deal out of it?"

Six weeks later it was over. Alasdair often mocked my dream to become a lawyer or an architect and to study at McGill or at the University of Toronto (U of T). One day, this ended in a huge fight. We split. Despite the breakup, I was happy. I now knew that it was possible for a boy to like me, and my father had made a major concession to Canadian culture.

Alasdair started dating Janet Riverton again. I wrote him a fatuous twelve-page letter in violet ink, criticizing his behaviour and character. I returned his ring and left it and the letter in his locker. Then I started seeing one of his best friends. The next day when I opened my locker, the ring was there, a tightly rolled note from Alasdair inside. "Keep it, I chose it for you."

مريم

Laurie and I went to the beach near my house after school. We stood on the rocks and watched the tide come in.

"He gave me back the ring. I don't want it. I really don't." I said to her.

"Throw it into the ocean," suggested Laurie.

I took the ring out of my coat pocket, looked at it one last time, and threw it as hard as I could. We watched the ring hit the water and then disappear.

مریم

"**M**y father hasn't met any of my boyfriends in thirty-four years," I explained to Eli, now my husband. "It's going to be weird."

"Are you nervous?" said Eli.

"No, I'm not nervous. It does feel strange to be bringing a man home in my fifties. I haven't had much practice."

My hand wobbled slightly as I turned the key and opened the door of my father's condo. Eli followed me inside. Papa and Eli shook hands. He gave my father a gift of tea. The three of us sat at the kitchen table. I realized Papa was sitting on the same chair where I sat on the day that I had asked permission to go on my first date. There were no martinis; the happy face glass was long gone. My mind was miles away as I tuned in and out of the conversation. "And what does your father do? Do you have any brothers and sisters?"

مریم

"**Y**ou seem different with your father," said Eli on the drive home. "A little tense."

I looked out the car window.

"I know. It felt very strange and new to be sitting in my father's kitchen with you. Papa never accepted any of my boyfriends. It's not like how your parents, who wanted to meet me, invited me over for dinner. My father is very uncomfortable with the idea of a boyfriend."

Eli said, "So he never really adopted Canadian ways. Every father knows his daughter will have boyfriends. So, your father did whatever he wanted but, for you, it's a different story."

"Yes, I suppose you're right. For years I've kept my relationships with men very private from my father. It was a coping strategy."

"I feel sorry for him. He was completely unaware of a major part of your life for all these years? How can a father not want to know the man his daughter is with? I don't get it."

"I realized a long time ago that my father feared I would lose my identity unless I was with a man who could maintain it, i.e., a secular Muslim."

Eli laughed. "You? Lose your identity? I don't think your father gives you enough credit – you have a very strong sense of who you are."

"Yes, I suppose you're right. I often feel that my father has never really noticed how I have changed since my teenage years. I was less self-assured. He still trots out the arguments about how I am ashamed of my background. I think he wanted a Pakistani daughter, not a Canadian one. I can't help feeling that I let Papa down by being Canadian. I think that for him I will always be that Ca-NA-di-an girl."

16

Blame it on QWERTY

Arbutus Junior Secondary School
~ Typing Certificate ~

This is to certify that **Mariam Pal**

has successfully completed Level **7** of **7** Levels
and has attained a rate of **58** correct words a minute.

Principal _____

Teacher *Elsie Farr.*

Date *June 1974*

"No way! Mummy, no! I already took typing in grade nine. I don't want to take Typing Ten! And shorthand, too? What do you think I want to be – a secretary?"

I glared at my parents across the dining room table, defiant.

Grade nine was winding down. Elective forms for grade ten were due the next day. One of my parents needed to sign. And now my mother thought I should take another year of typing. Even worse, Papa suggested that I take shorthand. I rather liked typing, but I didn't think I needed another course. And shorthand?!

My mother looked at me with a smile. "My dear girl, nobody wants you to be a secretary. Far from it. Although it is an honest job. But if you don't master typing then who is going to type out your PhD thesis?"

I was floored. I didn't know what to say. Nor could I think of a counterargument.

I stared at the yellow piece of paper on the dining room table. I could feel my parents looking at me.

After a long minute, I spoke.

"Well, okay, I'll take Typing Ten."

I became a very good typist. I completed all seven levels and attained a rate of fifty-eight correct words per minute, according to the "Typing Certificate" that I found in a file of my report cards maintained by my father. As a top student, I was allowed to use the school's one IBM Selectric typewriter. These stylish machines, still found in dusty corners of offices to this day, came in cool colours like bright blue, orange, and red. They literally purred when switched on and used a small removable typeball available in italic and other fonts.

I never followed my father's smart advice to learn shorthand. Had I done so, this skill would have helped me enormously in a professional lifetime spent taking notes.

Papa insisted that his daughters learn three practical life skills: swimming, driving, and touch-typing. He typed using the "hunt and peck" method, and though he clicked along at a respectable speed, he envied how my mother's hands flew across the keyboard.

My father never learned how to swim. His mother, like many Pakistanis, afraid that he would drown, kept him far away from water. Despite many opportunities as an adult, he never learned how to swim. But he did get a driver's license early on in his Canadian life.

Although delayed by a proclivity to ear infections, eventually I did learn how to swim, and I got my driver's license at sixteen. Typing classes started in junior high in grade nine. My typing, swimming, and driving skills have served me well and I am grateful to my father for ensuring that I acquired them at an early age. When they signed my electives form, my parents could never have predicted the far-reaching impact that my ability to type would have on my life. Neither could I. It opened the door to the world of work and financial independence.

I learned to type in the 1970s on a manual typewriter. The classroom at Arbutus Junior Secondary School was presided over by Mrs. Elsie Farr. A bubbly, diminutive British woman in Monty Python-esque floral dresses, she had an unbridled enthusiasm for typing. Seated at tables in rows of six or seven students, Mrs. Farr taught us how to change the ribbon, how to clean the typewriter, as well as the secrets of centering a title and other neat tricks. Decades later I still remember how to centre a line on a standard piece of paper.

Throughout my university studies, I typed my own term papers, saving me money. Memorizing the QWERTY keyboard prepared me for the twenty-first century. It also helped me get great summer jobs working for the Government of British Columbia.

مريم

It was the second to last day of high school and I was chatting with friends in the cafeteria. A crackling sound came from the speakers on the wall, indicating a P.A. announcement was forthcoming.

"Attention! Attention! Two students are needed to work at the Gordon Head Road crosswalk until the end of June. The pay is $50. Report to the school office immediately if you're interested."

The cafeteria was located immediately across from the school office. Seconds later I was at the reception. I had just got my first job. A club at my high school operated a crossing guard service for students at a nearby elementary school all year. Senior high finished earlier than elementary and two students were needed to continue the service for another week.

Three times a day I rode my bike up the hill from home to school where I picked up an orange safety vest and a stop flag on a pole. I joined the other student who had arrived at the office just behind me and the two of us worked the crossing for a week. That first fifty dollars gave me a taste of what it was like to have my own money. A couple of weeks later, on a family trip to Seattle, I bought a pair of platform sandals that I had been craving which Mummy refused to buy for me.

After my brief stint as a crossing guard, summer boredom quickly set in. Most of my friends had jobs so there was nobody to hang out with during the day. My mother always had very irritating things for me to do. I was sick of cleaning the silver or weeding the garden. I wanted paid work, preferably in an office.

Papa, not too keen on me working in the summers, wanted me to stay at home. He never explained why. Papa also made it clear that he would not allow me to take my mother's car (I was not allowed to drive his car) to any job that I managed to get. Furthermore, he disapproved of me working evenings and weekends. This meant a job at McDonald's, or waitressing, or any retail job was out.

So, I decided to get a job with the BC government. They paid well and the hours were a predictable 8:30 to 4:30 every day. Consequently, these jobs were difficult to get. Papa said I would never land a government gig. This made me more determined than ever. I went to the downtown student employment centre almost every day for a month hoping that I would find a job. The staff began to recognize me. I was polite, resolute, and consistent, and although I didn't realize it at the time, I was honing what would be my approach to the world throughout my life. I was better organized and more persistent than anybody else.

Finally, at the beginning of August, I received a call asking me to report to the Ministry of Public Works to fill in for vacationing staff for two weeks. The pay was $360. I was ecstatic.

Assigned to the office of the deputy minister, my first duty was learning to answer the telephone. At seventeen, I was remarkably confident and gregarious, but these characteristics totally failed me when it came to answering the office telephone.

"Okay, Mariam. So, here's what you do," explained Grace, the deputy minister's secretary. "When the telephone rings, make sure you have a message pad and pencil handy. When you answer you should say: 'Office of the deputy minister of public works! Good morning, how can I help you?'"

I nodded – it sounded easy. Then the phone started to ring. I picked up the receiver, opened my mouth, and nothing came out. I was absolutely tongue-tied; my hands were clammy, and I could feel my face turning bright red. Grace grabbed the phone from my hand and answered it. After she hung up, she looked at me and smiled.

"That's okay. Don't worry. It looks easier than it really is, right? Here, let's practice. Pretend the phone's ringing – ring ring!"

I picked up the receiver. I froze again. I wanted to sink into the floor. But the secretary was patient. Then I had a thought.

"I know what I'll do. I will write out what I have to say on a piece of paper and have it in front of me whenever I answer the phone."

"Well, that's a good idea," replied Grace.

Script in hand, my telephone answering skills quickly improved. The job was actually quite easy; both the deputy minister and his secretary were on vacation. In the days before voicemail and answering machines, a human presence was still needed. I answered, took messages, and tunneled through an enormous pile of filing. I loved everything about the job and was disappointed when the two weeks were up.

The next summer, the BC government created the Youth Employment Programme for students. I had just completed my first year at university. After registering and waiting for nearly a month for even one call to an interview that never came, I learned that some girls I knew whose fathers were well placed in the government had got great jobs. And they didn't even know how to type!

Furious, I sat down at my desk and typed a letter to the minister of labour. My copy was lost years ago, but I remember that I complained about nepotism and the generally rude and unhelpful attitude of the staff towards students. For good measure, I cc'd the letter to the leader of the opposition, two other party leaders, and the premier. The morning after I mailed the letter, I was called to an interview. I accepted the job, with the Ministry of the Environment, and started right away.

Several days later, the phone rang at ten o'clock at night. My mother answered the telephone. "Mariam Pal? She's gone to bed. This is her mother speaking. How can I help you?"

It was the minister of labour's assistant, wanting to speak to me. They called again the next morning, but I had already left for work. Finally, we spoke that evening. I received a sympathetic ear and assurances that things would change. Papa was angry with me for raising such a fuss, suggesting that I should have been more patient with the system. He was probably right.

From 1976 until 1981 I had a series of challenging summer jobs with the BC government. My glowing letters of reference described my work – I set up a library, typed ministers' letters, filed, answered the telephone, prepared a directory, catalogued historical records, and wrote a huge report on continuing education across the province. I learned about public administration, office organization, and getting along with people. The money was excellent and the hours regular.

Papa the pessimist, who had predicted that I would never get a government job, was not very happy with my working full-time all summer long. He and my mother both thought I should take a week or two to rest after finishing my exams, but I wanted to work. I know Mummy missed my company in the summers; I was no longer available to pick blackberries or make jam, but she understood my need for independence and new experiences much better than my father did. Papa was not interested in my work. Nor did he want to hear my office stories. I shared all this with my mother. But even Papa was impressed when he found out how much money I had saved.

Still, he complained endlessly and loudly.

"Mariam, why do you have to ride to work with that red-headed boy in his noisy sports car? It always wakes me up when he starts the engine."

"But Papa, Adam starts his engine every day whether or not I'm going with him in the car to work. And it's cheaper than taking the bus. You're always telling me to be careful with my money."

"You and your job, Mariam. You only think of yourself. You earn too much money now – you'll have to file your own income taxes. I can't claim you as my dependent anymore. Goddammit, I pay so much income tax already."

I sat in silence and did not reply. I didn't know what to say. I loved my jobs with the government and was very proud of what I had accomplished. I knew how much my father disapproved of my summer jobs. The fact that I earned too much money to be claimed as a dependent was not the real issue. My growing economic independence made it increasingly difficult for Papa to control me.

My good salary took me farther away from Papa's sphere of influence. For example, for years he had refused to pay for contact lenses. I bought them with my own money. The day that I came home wearing my first pair of contact lenses my father was furious at me. I had taken the later bus home because my optician's appointment was after work. I called my mother from the office to tell her I would be late. I brought home the Vancouver paper with me every night and reminded her to make sure my father knew that his paper would be late.

I walked in the door, delighted not to be wearing glasses. "Oh, come here, can I see them in your eyes?" said my mother. Papa stayed seated on the living room sofa, not even muttering hello behind his newspaper. He was not interested at all. I approached him. "Here is the Vancouver paper, Papa. I'm sorry it's late but I had an optician's appointment right after work."

Papa snarled in reply, "It's too late for the paper now. You can keep it." He put down the paper he was reading, gave me a withering look, got up, and left the room. He never mentioned my contact lenses again and questioned my reliability because I was late that one day with his newspaper. I had to beg and plead with him for the privilege of buying his paper again knowing that this meant I could never take a later bus from downtown. It was a way of controlling me. The following summer, the newsstand near the bus stop had closed. I was so relieved.

I was becoming less financially dependent on my parents and building my own life. I loved working in downtown Victoria. I felt so free, and I especially liked my lunch hours. I met my friends in the park at noon, occasionally went out to restaurants for lunch or dinner, browsed at one of Victoria's many bookstores, or went window-shopping around downtown. Victoria was not Montréal, but for a girl who'd spent most of her life in the suburbs, there was a lot to see and do.

مريم

When it was time to type my thesis, not for my PhD but for my MA, I was prepared. Mummy had been right.

My MA thesis, at 150 pages, would have been a long slog on my mother's portable Smith Corona manual typewriter that she had lent me several years before. Her old typewriter had been with me through several years at McGill, many term papers, and the version of my CV that got me my first professional job.

A new device called the personal computer was available to students in the Department of Economics. I booked one- and two-hour slots, gradually entering the text of my thesis in WordStar. I saved it on five-inch floppy disks. Once I got the hang of the keyboard and figured out the basics of word processing, I was hooked. There was no turning back from the world of computers. I started saving to buy one.

On my next trip home, I brought my mother's typewriter back to Victoria. Mummy watched her old typewriter in its matching hard case slide down the chute and onto the revolving luggage carousel. I was not prepared for the crestfallen look on her face. I didn't need her typewriter anymore. Technology and I had both moved on.

17

Auntie Cathreen

Middle Uncle, Mummy, Big Uncle, 1959

They were talking about me. As if I weren't there! Exactly what Mummy had warned me about. A few days prior to my departure we discussed my upcoming trip to Pakistan.

"Mariam, in Pakistan people will consider you a woman even though you are only eighteen. In Pakistan, it's the age where most girls get married."

"What do you mean?" I asked, baffled. "I don't want to get married!"

"Well, men – like your father's friends – will ignore you. When you were a child, it was all right for them to speak to you, but now that you are grown up, things are different."

Mummy continued, "I know, it's upsetting and even humiliating but you have to understand that they are being polite. Most Pakistani men are raised never to make eye contact with or talk to an unrelated woman. For them, being polite means ignoring you completely."

مریم

In Lahore, slouched in a huge, upholstered chair underneath the squeaky ceiling fan, I felt like part of the furniture. At home in Canada, my parents entertained regularly, and I was used to being part of the conversation. On my last visit to Pakistan, the ten-year-old me enjoyed talking with adults. But on that hot Lahore evening eight years later I had become invisible.

I hate this place, I thought. Papa sensed my discomfort.

"Just a few more minutes. Okay, Mariam?"

"Okay."

I was totally bored. Imprisoned in a hot room in the family house in Lahore, I listened to my father and his friends talking. From the little I understood, I knew the topic was Pakistani politics. And then I heard some words in English. My ears perked up.

"And what is she studying?" asked my father's friend. Papa swiftly replied, "She has just finished first year university and is going to major in sociology."

218

I felt a warm flush creep up my already hot face and took another sip of my Coke.

Mummy had given me one last piece of advice.

"Oh, and another thing. Some Pakistani men think they are modern and will offer their hand. My advice is to never shake hands with men in that country – they are lousy hand-shakers. It's like holding a wet fish." Mummy grimaced and I laughed. Later, when I was older and working in Pakistan, I always remembered – and heeded – her advice. Many men I met through my work seemed relieved when I did not insist on shaking hands.

A couple of days after my talk with Mummy, Papa and I left for Pakistan. From the moment we landed in Karachi, this trip was nothing like what I remembered from my childhood visits. Everywhere I went I was pulled aside and treated differently because I was female. As a child, Pakistan had seemed to be a place of incredible freedom because I could go to bed whenever I wanted and gorge on Fanta and cake. As an eighteen-year-old I was simply classified as a woman – and this was not good.

In Canada, I went through the airport security check knowing my father was behind me, but in Pakistan I had to go through the women's security line by myself. My handbag and carry-on were invariably selected for hand inspection. The female security agents exploited the situation by carrying out a curious inspection rather than one based on real security concerns. They opened up my lipsticks.

"Ayee! *Bohut* beautiful colours!"

The agent then spritzed a bit of my eau de toilette into the air. She sniffed appreciatively and smiled.

"*Shookria! Bas.* Finished."

I was too shy and too young to protest, and they knew it.

In time, I got smarter and checked my toiletries and cosmetics and filled my carry-on with shoes and dirty underwear. Security became a breeze.

At a Karachi hotel where my father and I checked in, the management assumed that I was his young bride and gave us the honeymoon suite. When Papa saw the gaudy gold-and-red decorations on the ceiling above the double bed, he was both disgusted and furious. He immediately went down to the reception to complain and have us put in a room with two twin beds. Later, he explained to me that from their perspective, the Pakistanis at the front desk of the hotel were perfectly reasonable to assume that a man in his early fifties married a teenage relative or the daughter of a family friend.

Papa's betrothal to a younger cousin had been arranged since childhood. His intended earned a degree in economics so she could understand his work. But my father had other ideas. As he wrote *Dada Abajee*, Papa wanted to get to know his future wife before deciding on marriage. In 1950s Pakistan most couples only met each other on their wedding day. My father's cousin was deeply shocked by his refusal to marry her and never wed.

Papa had a good time in Europe. He dated British girls and even had a girlfriend in Paris. When he arrived in Montréal in August 1955, Papa had already been married, to a British woman named Eileen. She followed him to Pakistan after Papa graduated from the London School of Economics. They married in Lahore but two years later she left for

London, unable to adapt to Pakistani life. She never returned and they divorced.

"You know, Mariam, I didn't want to marry again. But I did." Papa told me this several years after my mother's death. Marry again he did, this time to a Canadian.

مریم

Mummy's relationship with Pakistan began with a chance encounter at the main gate of the McGill University campus sometime in the spring of 1956. My parents had met a few weeks before. My mother, tagging along with friends, ended up at a party thrown by my father and his roommate at their apartment on McGill College Avenue in downtown Montréal. My father's apartment was steps away from the McGill gates. Mummy lived on nearby Durocher Street.

"She looked like Ingrid Bergman," said Papa. "So I asked her out."

Several months after they met, Papa moved to Ottawa to take up a position as an economist for the Canadian Good Roads Association. He and my mother wrote letters. My father bought a small car and drove back to Montréal on weekends. Mummy had a sister, Elizabeth, in Ottawa so she was there from time to time. Accounts vary but I'm fairly sure that my mother sent him a set of dishes as a gift. The dishes were a private joke between the two of them which went on for years.

"She was crazy about me," Papa would boast.

A year after they met, in the spring of 1957, my parents married in Ottawa. They soon returned to Montréal as my father wanted to finish his PhD in economics at McGill. Their plan was to return to Pakistan to live, assuming my father got a good job.

By the time she met my father, my mother had shed her small-town skin in favour of a more cosmopolitan one. She had lived in Toronto, Montréal, and London, England, read widely and voraciously, and was curious about the world. Writing to her closest friend, telling her that she is to be married – "... it's the man from Pakistan." Catherine further notes that "I feel a very deep affinity with his culture and perhaps being Slav it's understandable." Two years later, writing a few days after her arrival in Lahore, she writes, "I find a great number of things common to Slavs ..." I will never know what my mother meant when she equated Pakistani and Slavic culture but her openness to her husband's world was apparent.

The girl from Chapleau, Ontario, who had spoken only Polish for the first six years of her life, took a passionate interest in her husband's country of Pakistan with unconditional love, tempered by a critical and insightful understanding of this complex and ancient culture. It certainly helped that the family accepted her "on sight," as she wrote home to a friend. The whole clan, bearing garlands of white jasmine flowers, went to the Lahore Railway Station to meet her and me. Yet she only visited Pakistan four times in her life and never lived there.

Mummy was a keen observer of all that was around her. She picked up a few words in Punjabi and Urdu. Not speaking Punjabi, the *lingua franca* of the family house in Lahore, did not appear to be a barrier. Mummy observed and listened – the rise in pitch of someone's voice, a slight change in comportment signaled to her that something was up.

My mother developed a profound understanding of Pakistani society. Given her infrequent visits, her knowledge was all the more impressive. She helped me appreciate and understand many aspects and nuances of Pakistani life, particularly for women. She made no secret of her disgust regarding many cultural practices such as *purdah* (literally, this word means veiled), which refers to an extreme separation of men and women in daily life.

"So many Pakistani women are prisoners within their home, Mariam," she would say to me, "and it is men who put them there and keep them there."

Born in a different time, Mummy might have become a sociologist or an anthropologist. Culture fascinated her, particularly the treatment of women in different societies. Returning to university in her late forties, she was especially fascinated by the comparative study of women all around the world. She was excited by her studies and wanted to share her new knowledge. When I came home from school she was bursting with new information, but I was a bored, self-absorbed fifteen-year-old.

"The machismo of Japanese and Chinese men was extraordinary, Mariam. Did you know that in traditional Japanese and Chinese culture the doctor cannot examine a female patient? The woman lies on a bed behind a screen and her husband points at a chart of the human body, indicating where she feels pain."

I listened, bored. Another feminist history lesson. Why couldn't Mummy be a nurse or real estate agent like the other mothers I knew who worked? At least I understood what they did. Anthropology and women's studies did not interest me in the least.

Pretending not to notice my less than enthusiastic attitude, Mummy continued.

"You see, dear girl, men want to control women. And it's not just in Pakistan!"

"Pakistan is a man's world," she often said. She greatly admired my grandmother, *Ammi Jee*. According to Mummy, my grandmother had the most beautiful feet she had ever seen because she had never worn a pair of shoes in her life. This was not because of poverty, but rather due to the fact that she wore loose sandals all day long. In a household where men's needs always came first, *Ammi Jee* followed a lifelong habit of rising early in order to bathe and eat her breakfast before her husband and three sons. It was my mother who noticed something was wrong with her mother-in-law's eyes – she had developed cataracts, which were successfully operated on.

Mummy had strong opinions on other aspects of Pakistani culture. Sex for example. She thought the veneer of piety was a farce, telling me that it was impossible to suppress sex the way Pakistanis thought they were doing.

"Just look at women in Lahore. They wear the tightest, sexiest *shalwar kameezes* I have ever seen. Lots of cleavage, tight around the arms. Don't tell me it's a coincidence. Sex is always there, and Pakistanis are no different."

Mummy had the courage, on her first visit to Pakistan in 1959, to take a stand different from most of the family. A distant female cousin of my father's, who lived in Rawalpindi, had been kicked out by her new husband after a few months of marriage. Humiliated, the woman returned home to her parents. Mummy said all the Pals blamed the woman for the failed marriage. The distraught cousin was made fun of and derided by the family. Only my mother stood up for her, obviously feeling empathy for the cousin. Incredibly, my mother was eventually able to turn family opinion around.

My Pakistani family regards the woman they called Auntie Cathreen, my mother, as a legend. Her reputation has grown in the three decades since her death in 1987 at the age of just sixty-two. The first time I met my second cousin, Aziz, he asked me about her. He looked a bit confused.

"Did your mother speak Urdu? The way everyone talks about her, it's like she fit into the family perfectly!"

"No, she never learned Urdu, although she picked up a few words."

"Everyone speaks so highly of her; I wish I had known her."

His mother, my first cousin, has never forgotten playing dolls with Mummy in Lahore. Mummy has assumed almost a saintly status.

My cousin Hamza said, "She always seemed to know Pakistan better than the Pakistanis. I remember Auntie Cathreen making my father take her to the archeological ruins at Harappa. I thought it was boring but if it hadn't been for her, I never would have known about this place."

"Ah, yes Hamza, I think I remember now. It was just after Mummy had returned to university in her forties. She had devoured an anthropology course and was thrilled when she learned the ruins of the ancient Indus Valley civilization were located within a few hours' drive of Lahore." I continued, "She couldn't understand why I didn't take more interest in a couple of rocks that she brought from there. But I was thirteen years old, and anthropology did not interest me in the slightest."

Mummy was a dedicated correspondent; she wrote regularly for decades to my grandfather, her father-in-law, with news of his youngest son and two granddaughters. Her letters were eagerly anticipated at the family home, No. 1 Fane Road in Lahore, where they would be read and simultaneously translated by *Dada Abajee* into Kashmiri or Punjabi as he read them aloud to my grandmother or other (mostly female) relatives who did not speak English. After her first visit in the summer of 1959, my mother started writing letters to her father-in-law and two brothers-in-law.

Mummy's letters chronicle the history of my family. They bulge with anecdotes any grandparent would love to hear – the first steps, first shoes, and first words. While the contents were not particularly exciting, they were well written, and she had the ability to spin a mundane day's activities into a charming story. She clearly enjoyed corresponding with her relatives in Pakistan. It must have been painful for her when this communication stopped, first with Big Uncle in the early '70s and then with her father-in-law in the mid-'70s. My father, the scrappy youngest son, was fighting hard with his father and elder brother over his right to inherit valuable land in Lahore. My grandfather lost his connection to his two Canadian granddaughters when the letters stopped.

Decades later, I sat in my dining room reading the letters. My mother was always doing something to try to help her family in Pakistan. She sent salt substitute for *Ammi Jee*, who suffered from high blood pressure, and metal ice cube trays in time for the hot season. In one letter Mummy enclosed some seeds and instructed her father-in-law to ask the gardener to plant them soon. They were Ontario blue grape seeds and Mummy wanted to be sure the plant was thriving before my parents moved back to Lahore. At least that was the plan. There was warm underwear for her parents-in-law in a particularly damp and cool Lahore winter, and Pears soap for *Dada Abajee's* sensitive skin. She seemed to know what everybody needed. Sometimes she got it wrong. After receiving a couple of shipments of *Chatelaine* magazine for his wife, Big Uncle wrote to her in the nicest way to tell her not to send these magazines anymore. The photographs of Western women showing their legs and other body parts were not going down well in the family. She promptly stopped sending them.

Mummy was also imaginative, sending dried maple leaves, carefully pressed in wax paper between the pages of her dictionary, to be put on the family graves.

When I read my mother's letters to her Pakistani relatives, I was astounded at her encyclopedic knowledge of the Pal family. It reminded me of how she would ask a million questions when my father and I returned from trips to Pakistan in 1969, 1977, and 1980.

"How is Qaleem?" she asked, and before my father had a chance to respond, out shot the next question. "What about Burree-bee, is she still alive?" These questions continued for days as my mother remembered one relative or another, or some of my father's friends. I heard them talking about people in the middle of the night when they were in bed and also while they had their morning tea in the kitchen. I wish I had listened but news about people I didn't know who lived far away didn't interest me.

Mummy mastered the family tree. This seems remarkable to me because she did not speak the language. Moreover, it cannot have been easy to remember so many unfamiliar names, many of which were impossible for her to pronounce properly. I think that she must have written down and then studied the names of the relatives and friends that she was meeting over the course of the summer of 1959. As a former amateur actress, perhaps she used skills learned in the theatre to help her memorize and learn her family lines.

When Auntie Cathreen died in 1987, there was a brief thaw between the three feuding brothers. They had all loved her and were shocked by her early death. United in sorrow, both Middle Uncle and Big Uncle wrote their younger brother sincere and touching letters of sympathy.

18

Turn off that noise

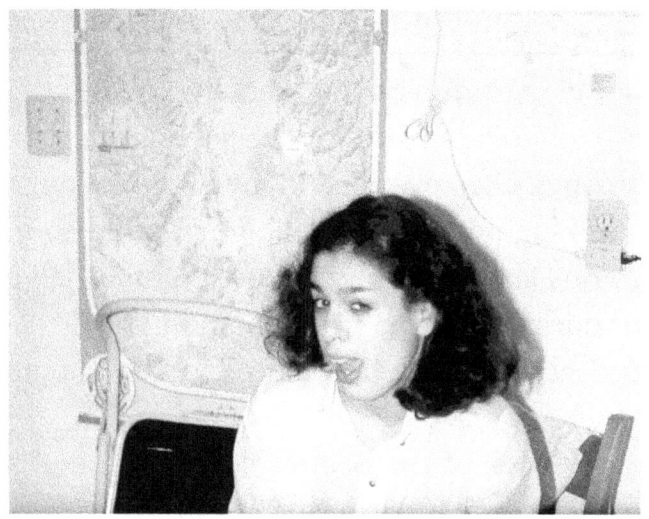

Mariam, 1980

"That'll be $2.99!" cried the cashier. He slipped my record into a psychedelic orange-and-purple plastic bag and placed it on the counter.

"Who'll stop the raaaiiinnnn..." howled Creedence Clearwater Revival. The music at A&B Sound was so loud I could hardly hear him. But I thought it was great. It was 1970, I was downtown by myself, the Beatles had broken up (it was all Yoko's fault), and I was in a record store buying my first album!

I took three one dollar bills out of my wallet and laid them on the counter. Proudly clenching my purchase, I walked out of the shop.

An hour before, I had hopped off the bus and walked to A&B Sound, Victoria's biggest record store. I made a beeline to the Beatles section and flipped through the discs – *Sgt. Pepper*, *Magical Mystery Tour*, *Revolver*. They were all four or five dollars each.

"Oh no! I didn't bring enough money!" I held back tears. I had saved five dollars from my weekly allowance; this was the most money I had ever had in my wallet in my entire life. It was not enough. I wanted an album, but I also needed to pay for my bus fare home and hoped to get myself a treat to snack on during the bus ride home. There had to be something I could afford. I couldn't go back home empty-handed.

At the very back of the Beatles section I found an album called *Very Together*. It was just $2.99. I had never heard of it. None of the songs were familiar but the names were. The cover featured a photo of a candelabrum. Three candles burned and above the fourth candle, just extinguished, floated silvery white smoke. This album was recorded in 1960 when the Beatles were a Hamburg bar band.

I was thrilled to be going home with a Beatles album. But I was broke. I had my bus fare home (twenty-five cents) and enough to buy a small bag of caramel popcorn (fifty cents) at The Nut Shoppe on Yates Street. This left me with a dollar for the week's necessities: a new radio battery (nineteen cents at Radio Shack) and the occasional fudgesicle (fifteen cents). As I stood waiting for the bus, not scheduled to arrive for another half hour, I decided it was time to negotiate a raise in my allowance. How else would I afford to buy more Beatles records?

I was dying to get home and listen to my purchase. The problem was that we didn't have a stereo. An ancient mono record player was built into our old black-and-white television cabinet in the TV room downstairs. Mummy used to play her *Zorba the Greek* or Herb Alpert albums on it. A couple of years earlier, my father had put our brand-new colour television on top of the cabinet. It was Saturday, which meant my parents went downstairs after dinner to watch Merv Griffin or a movie. If I got home early enough, I might be able to listen to my album once or maybe twice before I had to set the table and eat dinner. That would be it until Sunday. It all depended on whether or not my father was working in his study next to the TV room. Why didn't my parents get a stereo?

My badgering paid off. Mummy started stereo shopping. She refused to buy components. A stereo, like the big old radio receivers she had grown up with in the 1930s, should look like a piece of furniture. One day I came home from school and there it was, a huge, pecan wood trunk with a stereo inside. It was like a musical tank, only made of wood. Hinged doors with decorative clasps covered the massive speakers and had to be opened whenever music was played. A hinged top opened to reveal a turntable, a tuner, and a place to store records. The entire monstrosity was on casters, supposedly to make it easier to move, although I couldn't understand why anybody would want to do so.

I moved my growing collection of records into the living room and camped out there for hours at a time. My mother, I now realize, was slowly going nuts listening to my music. One night at dinner, a couple of weeks after music arrived at our house, Mummy made two announcements. The first was that she was taking a music appreciation course.

"I think it's time I learn about other forms of music besides serious music."

"Serious music?" I said. "Mummy, you are so condescending. The Beatles and Mick Jagger are serious musicians."

My mother looked at me thoughtfully.

"Yes, I suppose they are serious musicians too. I was thinking about classical music. People study for many years to master an instrument. But hold on, there's something else . . ."

"*Izzmia*," she said, using Papa's family nickname, "we need some headphones. Mariam is always listening to music. I must have my peace and quiet. Tomorrow is payday. Will you please . . ." Her voice trailed off the way it always did when she was tired. Papa understood. He silently nodded his head.

A day later Papa arrived home with a big pair of headphones and a long extension cord, tightly coiled like a telephone cable.

"Here you go, Mariam," he said as he put the box on the kitchen table. "At last, there will be some peace and quiet in this house. I paid a lot for these earmuffs."

"Papa!" I said. "Jeez. They're headphones, not earmuffs." But I don't think my father was listening.

My father always called them earmuffs. I think he did it just to bother me.

مریم

Papa had absolutely no appreciation for music. I cannot recall him ever enjoying listening to a song. And he had a particularly low tolerance for my music. Entering a room where I was playing the radio or the stereo, he would always grimace and bark, "Turn off that noise!"

Yet Papa was remorseful that he didn't learn to appreciate music while growing up. He always said it was too late for him to learn. He'd been raised in a household where music was equated with sinful behaviour. Instruments were played and songs were sung by dancing girls in *Heera Mandi*, Lahore's red-light district, not by my father and his brothers. I was well into my twenties before I discovered Pakistani music and realized just how oblivious my father was of his culture's rich musical traditions.

There were no piano lessons for me; my mother's view of music forming part of a well-rounded education was overruled. A few years later, Papa had mellowed; my sister studied the violin for a little while until she got bored with playing an instrument that was not really her choice.

Mummy loved the music appreciation course. To my great irritation, she always wanted to share what she had learned with me.

"Guess who we heard today, Mariam – Frank Zappa and the Mothers of Invention! Did you know he named one of his children Moon Unit? And what was their name – oh yes, the Rolling Stones? Very interesting. I never had any idea what they were singing about until I took this course."

Mummy thought that music appreciation was a two-way street.

"If I listen to the Beatles and the Rolling Stones, then I think you should try listening to music I love. Fair's fair, right?"

Reluctantly, I agreed. And that is how my sister and I found ourselves slumped in enormous chairs in a dark living room listening to opera on the stereo. I hated it as much as my mother reveled in it. Then Mummy's friend's husband fell fast asleep and started snoring in the middle of *Carmen*. That was the end of our opera afternoon.

In my bedroom, I had both a portable transistor and a clock radio. I was ecstatic if a song I really liked came on. Papa bought me the small transistor radio for my twelfth birthday. He was fed up with my "borrowing" the little radio he kept in the bathroom so he could listen to the news while shaving. My new radio had a matching black leatherette case with a strap so that I could carry it around. I was always listening to the radio whose dial was cemented to CKLG from Vancouver. CKL-GEE! They played the hits and I listened, glued to my radio. My batteries were always running down because I would fall asleep listening to the radio. I still do.

I knew all the names of the disc jockeys on CKLG. I loved all their corny jokes and felt like they were my friends. When I found out that CKLG's top DJ, Roy Hennessey, was making a guest appearance at the local Kmart, I begged my mother to take me and bless her heart she did. But once I got there, I joined the other teenage girls milling around Kmart's cosmetic department, too shy to approach him. I left without the autograph.

I longed to phone in a song request to CKLG so I could hear my name on the air. Back then, long distance telephone calls, even to Vancouver, were expensive and I didn't dare call. I entered lots of contests, mainly to win albums, but never got lucky. Just before Christmas 1970, CKLG announced a new contest. It was a little different. Listeners were asked to send in their name and the name of their best friend. If their best friend's name were drawn, they would receive a copy of George Harrison's post-Beatles album called *All Things Must Pass* for Christmas. I didn't have a best friend who could give my name, but I desperately wanted to enter, so I made up a name using the first and last names of two friends. I sent in my entry and waited for news, hoping that this time I would win. Just before Christmas, I came home from school and saw a big box on the kitchen table addressed to me. The box was the size of a record album and the return address was CKLG's. Inside was the album and a form letter wishing me a Merry Christmas from my friends at CKLG and my best friend Lorraine Evans!

Throughout my teens, I faithfully read *Rolling Stone* magazine from cover to cover. I followed the breakup of the Beatles and the antics of the Rolling Stones avidly; acquiring all sorts of useless knowledge such as that Bianca Jagger married Mick in a wedding dress designed by Yves St. Laurent. And like all of us, I hated Yoko Ono for breaking up the Beatles. I had a huge poster of George Harrison above my bed and a picture of Mick Jagger taped to the mirror of my French provincial dresser. I loved reminding Papa that Jagger had studied at the London School of Economics – just like my father!

My parents, blissfully unaware of rock and pop music, only listened to CBC Radio from Vancouver. Daily, the CBC played a pop song right after the eight o'clock morning news. Elton John, Queen, and the Doobie Brothers all streamed into our kitchen on those 1970s mornings. I never left for school until I'd heard that day's tune. If the CBC featured a song I really loved, I turned up the volume and reveled at the invasion of my world into my parents' kitchen, until one of them would turn it down. I was excited when I discovered that my boyfriend Guy's parents also listened to CBC in the morning. We weren't the only ones! Many days Guy waited at the corner for me, then we rode or walked our bikes the rest of the way to school.

"Did you hear *Benny and the Jets* right after the news?" said Guy as we slowly biked up the hill. He started to sing "B-B-Benny and the jets . . ." Trailing behind him, a little out of breath, I smiled and nodded my head.

مریم

Mummy and Papa had been to a party the night before. Mummy showed us a mimeographed piece of paper with the words to a song.

"We all live in a uni-ver-si-ty, a uni-ver-si-ty . . ." She hummed along to a familiar tune.

"Aren't those students talented? Such a catchy tune!"

"Mummy, don't you know anything?" I groaned.

"They didn't write that music – that's the Beatles song *Yellow Submarine*. Everybody knows that song. You know, you should try listening to another radio station besides the

CBC. I can't believe you didn't recognize it. Look! I have the album right here."

"I thought it sounded familiar."

Papa put down the newspaper he was reading, looked up, and said, "The Beatles? Aren't those the men with the shaggy hair?" Then he went back to his newspaper.

Various albums and songs mirror the trajectory of my life. At eighteen, unhappily trudging through my first year of university, I came home every afternoon and blasted David Bowie's *Aladdin Sane* and *Ziggy Stardust* into the headphones. In my last year at the University of Victoria, before I left for McGill and Montréal, the album that got me through it all was Joni Mitchell's *Court and Spark*. Decades later, the music still resonates with me, hurtling me back to Victoria and memories of my profound unhappiness.

In Montréal, my musical horizons expanded as I learned about jazz and opera and attended a range of concerts from Stompin' Tom Connors to Ella Fitzgerald to Stevie Wonder. There was plenty of dancing in the McGill pub, at downtown clubs, and at gay bars.

Living abroad, I learned to dance the *quassa quassa* in West Africa, attended Indonesian *Gamelan* orchestra concerts, collected CDs of Pakistani music, and heard the delightful birdsong of temple bells in Bhutan.

I no longer have a stereo – I digitized all my CDs several years ago and I have no idea what happened to my headphones. My music is available to me at the click of a button on my phone. I have held on to some relics I cannot bear to part with: Michael Jackson's 1984 *Thriller* cassette tape, cassettes from Pakistan and Senegal, favourite LPs like

Janis Joplin's *Pearl* and a forty-five rpm LP of Don Maclean's *American Pie*, purchased at Eaton's basement in Victoria.

مریم

Papa never got the beat and lived a life bereft of music. Even the irresistible and infectious pulsations of a Punjabi *banghra* could not move him. After he retired, I tried taking him to a concert or two. After a rousing gospel recital, his main observation was about the historical development of gospel that he had read about in the concert programme and not about the music.

My father used to come to have dinner at my house. If music was playing, Papa would look at me, somehow managing to scowl, implore, and smile at the same time.

"Mariam, can you turn off that noise?" I always did what he asked even though it was my home. It was easier than a confrontation.

I had the last laugh. I married a musician.

19

The Boyfriend Club (II)

Mariam, 1979

Where do you find a suitable Muslim man if you haven't liked any of the ones you met at McGill or in Pakistan? Her father insists that they are around. Where? In the cabbage patch?
- **Letter from my mother to a friend, April 17, 1986.**

"And what does this man do for a living, Mariam?" said Papa. He glared at me.

"He's a lawyer. McGill law. He was in the same class as my friend Beth."

"And what about his parents – what do they do, and where are they from?"

I was beginning to feel nervous.

"Well, his mother's Portuguese and his father's Dutch. Both are professors. Like you. But in Toronto."

Papa was quiet. I could hear my own breathing. An ambulance, its siren blaring, roared down nearby Sherbrooke Street.

He looked at me and hissed, "Ah, so that means Christian grandchildren?"

I knew better than to reply. The conversation was over.

Disappointed, but not surprised; I had no logical reason to think Papa's long-standing hostile attitude towards my boyfriends had changed. For him, a Friday night movie date or a steady boyfriend were both just steps away from marriage. My having anything more than necessary contact with the opposite sex made him uncomfortable. Despite a lifetime in Canada, his upbringing in a gender-segregated culture ran strong and deep. It was an extraordinary attitude for a secular Muslim. I never saw him pray, fast during *Ramadan*, wear traditional Pakistani clothes, or any other indication that he was the slightest bit religious. If he felt uncomfortable that I went to school with boys, he never said so.

Papa was a good father. He instilled in me the value of hard work and responsibility, took me on international trips, helped me with my homework, and always encouraged me to do my best. When I said I wanted to be an architect or a lawyer, he didn't discourage me. Other fathers took their sons to hardware and gardening stores. Papa took me. Never once did I feel that Papa loved me any less because I was a girl and not a boy. On trips to Pakistan, old friends and relatives would offer to pray for him to have a son. Never hesitating for a second, Papa quickly assured them he was not pining for a boy.

It was not always easy having him as my father – he could be petty, stubborn, and self-absorbed. For more than forty years, my father and I disagreed vehemently on a fundamental issue. Papa insisted on a Muslim son-in-law. I wanted to marry whomever I wanted, like daddy did.

Each of us took a stand from which we refused to budge. Papa felt he had conceded enough; by Pakistani standards, he thought he was actually very liberal. My position was, and still is, that he had no right to demand that I marry a Muslim. This frustrated and angered both of us. Over the decades, Papa and I stumbled from one skirmish to another. My father castigated me for what he claimed was my lack of respect, impatience, and stubbornness.

"You know, Mariam, I was always honest with my own father. I would sit down with him, or write him a letter, and respectfully make my case. Maybe you should try my approach."

Papa's sanctimonious tone really got under my skin.

"But I am NOT Pakistani! I can't behave like you. I don't know how," I would shout in frustration.

The first serious indication that something was off with Papa and boys came in grade eight. I was thirteen. Out of the blue, Rob Bettas invited me to the fall dance. I thought it was a bit weird because I hardly knew him. Still, I asked Mummy if I could go. She checked with Papa and the answer was no. The refusal didn't really bother me – I was not too crazy about going with Rob anyway.

By the time I was in grade eleven, all I wanted to do was to go out with my friends, have fun at the dances, and get a boyfriend. Papa's opposition to my social life intensified.

I wore him down. Finally, at age sixteen, I got permission to go on my first date and to three dances a year.

The first three boyfriends took part in the awkward "meet my parents" pantomime. In hindsight, these must have been excruciating for Papa. I certainly didn't enjoy them. After meeting boyfriend number three, he had enough, declaring that he was no longer available. We agreed on rules. I could go out once a week and my curfew was midnight. After high school, my curfew was extended till 1 a.m.

In Papa-land, my Mr. Right should be secular so that father and son-in-law could enjoy martinis together while chit-chatting about politics. My intended should be Kashmiri. It would be even better if his family had moved to Lahore from Amritsar during Partition. A Pakistani of Punjabi, Sindhi, or other background could *potentially* be okay. Perhaps an Indian Muslim if he was from the north. A Bengali? Maybe in a pinch.

Papa's fundamental rationale was that I would lose the Canadian Muslim identity he had branded me with unless I did as he said. Weak and insecure, I would soon be sucked into attending church on Sundays, singing in the choir, and organizing the Christmas bazaar. Papa always used Christianity in his speculations, never any other religion. His premise derived from the unfortunate assumption that women forsake their identity when they marry. That is why all Pakistani brides look sad; they're leaving their family forever.

What it all boiled down to was that Papa married whom he wanted but I could not. Over the years, he convinced himself that he mellowed, that he was reasonable. After strenuous objections from Mummy, he reasoned, had he not abandoned his dream of arranging a marriage for me with a good Kashmiri boy? This was, in his mind, a huge shift. Papa simply did not see his hypocrisy.

"Mariam, if you compare me to other South Asian fathers, you'll see how far I have come in terms of my own culture," Papa used to say.

"But I live in Canada, not in Pakistan. And so do you."

"Values and questions of identity are universal, my dear girl," replied Papa.

Papa's position was all the more exasperating given that he dated and eventually married not one, but two women, of his choice. One was English and the other, my mother, Canadian. I wondered if he had ever told his father about his girlfriends. When Papa died, he left behind hundreds of letters to his father. The correspondence was in Urdu but with the help of some friends translating for me I was able to understand a few of them.

Reading his letters home, it was obvious my grandparents were not happy with their youngest son's ideas about love and marriage. Writing to my grandfather, *Dada Abajee*, a year after arriving in Canada, Papa was adamant in his refusal to enter into an arranged marriage. He would not take a bride sight unseen. His father assured his son that things had changed. Perhaps the two families could meet for tea? Papa said no. What my grandfather could not have known was that his son was already courting the woman who would become my mother. Mere days after his May 3, 1957 wedding, he wrote his father a bland letter about the weather and his studies. Papa told his parents about his marriage five months after it took place. I wonder if Mummy knew this.

مریم

In the fall of 1980, I left Victoria to attend McGill. I was ecstatic to be in Montréal. I loved everything about McGill. I felt free and in charge of my life.

At McGill I met other students with South Asian parents. It was a revelation. I had never known anyone in Victoria who could relate to my situation. These girls joked about it!

McGill's diversity amazed me. Everyone seemed to speak at least one other language. They were all so stylish. In letters home, I gushed about my experiences, my happiness jumping off the page.

Then there were the guys. Sharp, good-looking, and charming. And many of them, more than I had imagined, were Muslim. Papa's demands didn't seem so crazy. Maybe I could find a nice Muslim guy at McGill.

I studied hard and played hard. In the spring of 1981, I started dating a cute Palestinian. Enormously pleased with myself, of course I told my parents! He was smart, funny, and Muslim. Or at least that's what I thought. That's when I learned that some Palestinians are Christian. Oops. Papa hit the roof. He threatened to cut me off financially if I had any more boyfriends, Muslim or not, before finishing my degree. His rage was impressive. I took him seriously.

I went home to Victoria for the summer after my first year at McGill. Back at school in the fall, my romance with the Christian Palestinian had faded. Soon I was in the swing of my second year.

Papa's threat loomed, but he also lived at the other end of the country. Unless he hired a private detective, I knew there was only so much he could find out about my life. Halfway through my second year, I started dating a fellow economics student. He was Canadian, born in Taiwan. I did not tell my family, although Mummy figured it out. She knew enough not to tell Papa.

When this romance ended badly, I devoted my life to my MA thesis, the debating union, and pursuing my career in international development. I took a sabbatical from boys. I hung out with gay guys and had a lot of fun, finished grad school, and started to work. Papa and I enjoyed two years of relative peace.

By the mid-'80s, I'd not been in the boyfriend club for a while. When a friend in Europe sent a Frenchman, based in Paris, my way, I was ready. The Frenchman had regular business in Montréal, so we saw each other often. Before deciding to get more serious, I wanted to see him in his natural habitat. This seemed sensible to me. A frequent flyer points sale helped. I had enough to spend part of April in Paris!

There was one problem. I spoke regularly on the phone with my parents. I felt a sense of responsibility. I could not simply disappear.

After thinking about what to do, I wrote Papa. I told him about the Frenchman and explained why I had decided to go visit him in Paris. I hoped Papa would respect my sincerity and honesty and realize that I had grown up.

I must have been crazy. Papa exploded. He canceled my American Express card (I had a supplementary card through him) and ceased all contact with me. He then wrote me a letter detailing how much money he had spent on my education and demanded repayment. I applied for my own American Express card and was issued one several weeks later. As for the letter, I never replied. I remained in touch with Mummy.

I had a grand time in Paris. Two days after returning to Montréal I started a new job. On my first day at work, I was at the office until midnight. The next morning, I woke up with a fever, feeling dreadful. It was measles; although vaccinated, my injection had been an early version of the vaccine that had a fifteen percent failure rate. The incubation time pointed to Europe. And I had pneumonia. A "super infection," said the doctor.

I was ordered to quarantine for a week in my diminutive downtown apartment. Friends who had measles as children and were therefore immune brought me food. The Public Health Department checked on me daily. I was home sick for two weeks. Mummy called. Papa did not.

Mummy planned to come to Montréal in early June for my MA graduation ceremony. Worried about my health, she decided to stay an extra week. By then I was back at work, recovered but fragile. I was thrilled to come home to her dinners. Papa remained silent, never congratulating me on my new job or on getting my master's degree.

By the fall, it was over with the Frenchman. I went to work in Lahore on a project until the end of the year. With Mummy as intermediary, Papa informed my uncle and cousins that I would be coming to Lahore for work. But we never spoke directly.

Two months later, my project work completed, I arrived in Victoria via Lahore and Amsterdam on Christmas Eve. The last person I expected to see at the airport was Papa. But there he was, a big smile on his face as if nothing had happened. Mummy confirmed that he was impressed with my newfound enthusiasm for Lahore and Pakistan. All was seemingly forgiven. Perhaps he heard wedding bells?

Pakistan had made me giddy. My suitcases bulged with purchases from the bazaar, and I couldn't stop talking about all the interesting people I had met. Although he never said so, I could tell Papa was enormously pleased by my newfound knowledge of, and enthusiasm for, Pakistan. I never told him about the parties.

مریم

After Papa's reaction to the Dutch-Portuguese lawyer boyfriend, I realized that there was nothing to be gained by telling him about any man unless I planned to marry him. Mummy had always advised me to date whomever I wanted. Once I had met my future spouse, it would be time to tell my father.

"Your Papa will have to accept him."

This is more or less what I did.

Papa knew little of my private life. He rarely asked. When he did, it was always in an accusatory tone of a parent rebuking a misbehaving child.

I flirted with marriage to a South American when I lived in Manila. Breaking the news to Papa, it was clear he was not happy. I desperately wanted to talk to him as a mature daughter to her father, but Papa invariably reverted to the same tone he used when I was sixteen. By now in my forties, I found it tiresome being talked to like I was a teenager. I had survived several breakups and felt I had grown and matured. I longed for Papa to accept me and treat me like an adult.

What was really fascinating about my father was his ability to appear liberal and tolerant to most of the world. At times, his openness surprised me. I was taken aback to find out that his relationship advice was highly valued.

On Saturdays, for many years, Papa liked to go to a British style pub downtown for a Guinness. Occasionally, I joined him. The bartender was a pleasant young woman named Elizabeth.

"You know, your dad is really cool," she said to me on a frigid January evening when Papa went off to use the bathroom.

"What do you mean?" I answered, masking my surprise.

"He really listened when I told him about the problems my boyfriend and I were having. Boy, is he one smart cookie. You're lucky to have a dad like that to talk to."

Before I could reply, Papa was standing beside me, buttoning up his coat and fretting about the traffic.

A few months later, I was over at his condo for Sunday dinner.

"So, Papa, what have you been doing the last few days?" I asked, expecting the usual grousing about food shopping and how badly people parked in the grocery store parking lot.

"Well, I went to a wedding yesterday."

Papa at a wedding? He hated any and all ceremonies, be they graduations, weddings, or funerals.

"You've got to be kidding. Whose wedding?"

Papa smiled and took the lid off the chicken simmering on the stove. I could smell the fragrant spices of Lahore perfume his Montréal kitchen.

"It was Elizabeth – that woman from the pub downtown. Very nice wedding. Not too religious. Husband seems like a nice man."

After Papa died, I found a thank you note from Elizabeth in one of his files. His wedding gift had been "very generous and much appreciated." I wonder what he gave them.

I also found it remarkable that my father, who had grown up in a very homophobic environment, was so accepting of gay people.

Papa became friends with a helpful librarian at McGill. I knew Brian and that he was gay. The two of them went out for lunch from time to time.

"So, Papa, how was your lunch with Brian?"

Papa looked up from his newspaper and shook his head. "Brian is such a nice man. But you know, for someone in his situation it's difficult to find a partner. I feel bad for him."

Astonished, I did not reply.

Papa was not very interested in meeting or getting to know my friends. He was slightly more enthusiastic if they were of South Asian origin. I was surprised that he got along well with one of my very good friends, a gay man named Ian.

But for the most part they did not interest him any more than my boyfriends did.

Mummy died in 1987, years before I ever considered marrying anybody. I knew she disagreed profoundly with Papa's views on his daughters' marriages. Decades later, when I read some of her letters to a dear friend, she said he was unrealistic and authoritarian. Papa's duplicity angered and frustrated her. I think she felt helpless that she was unable to influence him more.

When I lived in West Africa, Papa and I met in London for a week's vacation. We stayed at the house of an old friend of his. K.K. was an eccentric, OCD-suffering, agoraphobic Pakistani historian. He never left the house and wore the same bathrobe over a fresh shirt and knee socks for the entire visit. During the day, Papa and I explored the London of his LSE days in the 1950s. Evenings, we dined with K.K. and his wife. I enjoyed listening to the discussions around the table.

One evening, talk turned towards intermarriage between cultures and religions. Papa started explaining how much Canada had changed. I listened, incredulous, as he talked admiringly about the Jewish community. In his opinion, Jews had adopted a realistic, accepting approach to interfaith marriage. I'm glad I was sitting down when he then declared that Pakistanis and other South Asians had their head in the sand when it came to such matters. I chose not to confront him. I knew this trip was special and did not want to ruin it.

Ironically, Mummy prevailed. I married a man of my choice when I wanted and how I wanted. Eli laughed when I explained to him that my father was concerned that I would lose my identity.

"You? Lose your identity? He must be crazy. Anybody can see that you have an incredibly strong sense of who you are. Maybe he needs new glasses."

What's really fascinating is why a man as intelligent and as liberal as my father held onto such restrictive and traditional views. I have my own theory. On some level, Papa felt that he let his family down by not marrying a Kashmiri and continuing with the family line. He therefore sought redemption through me. He wanted me to do what he was neither able nor willing to do.

I was forty-nine when I met Eli. I kept it pretty quiet but somehow Papa figured it out. He confronted me with his "suspicions" like I was a teenager caught in a lie. I refused to get into the same old discussion with him. By then I was so much smarter. I didn't really care when he refused to meet Eli for three years, invoking various flimsy reasons.

When I told him that we were moving in together, Papa didn't say much. By then he knew that the old drivel about my weak identity was not going to work so he didn't even try. When he finally met him, I think he kind of liked Eli. They even shared a few martinis together.

When we decided to get married, Eli went and spoke to Papa first. There were no in-laws to meet because Eli's parents had both died by then. Gertie, Eli's mother, was a strong woman. I would have liked to have seen Papa and her interact but never got the chance.

As the date of the wedding ceremony approached, my father became increasingly obstreperous and cantankerous.

He demanded to see a schedule for the wedding day. It was sent immediately. His pious reply that the *hora* dancing we had planned to start off the reception was not part of his culture. The implication was that dancing was sinful. I guess Papa had lived in Canada for so long that he had forgotten about the infectious and energetic *Bhangra* dancing, a highlight of most Pakistani weddings.

Invoking his health, Papa declined to attend the pre-wedding dinner or wedding reception because he couldn't sit for so long. He didn't offer to make any financial contribution. I was sad for him. No longer embarrassed by his behaviour, I didn't argue or try to convince him to participate more. I didn't say anything when he had the energy to travel four hours to and from Ottawa the weekend before and down to Vermont a few weeks after the wedding. I just kept quiet.

Papa squandered a huge opportunity by adopting the stance that he did. Our relationship as father and daughter matured in many ways but his stubborn refusal to consider anything but a Muslim son-in-law built a wall between us for most of my life.

While others benefited from his relationship advice and wise counsel, I never did. What I did get was Papa's support as I pursued my education and throughout some bumpy periods in my career. When an employer was treating me unfairly, it was Papa who told me I had to stand up for myself. He could be incredibly loyal and helpful, and I learned a lot from him. I remember how alone I felt my first few months in Abidjan and the good advice (read more, be patient) Papa gave me. When I discovered my maid had stolen from me, having grown up with servants, he understood how tough it was for me to fire her.

Papa once told me something that was very revealing and insightful.

"No man worth his salt will accept being treated the way I will act towards any boyfriend of yours who does not meet my criteria."

He was almost right. A parting shot from many of the men I dated was a remark about how my father would never accept them.

Eli toppled this house of cards with one pithy observation.

"No, Mariam, your father's attitude doesn't particularly bother me. We don't even know each other. It's got nothing to do with me. I'm willing to get to know him but he's got a problem. You're the one I want to spend time with, not your father. If he chooses not to have anything to do with me, I'm fine with it. It's not my preference, but if that's what he wants, then so be it."

Hmmm. Not bad for the cabbage patch.

20

Next stop, university

Mummy, 1984

"Where did you get that Trudeau button, Mummy?" I shouted towards the kitchen.

My mother sprinted down the hallway. She was in her yellow-and-black check Marimekko dress, which she only wore for special occasions. What was up?

"I went downtown," she panted, "to see Mr. Pierre Elliot Trudeau. It was really something, Mariam."

"You saw Mr. Trudeau?" I squealed. My jaw dropped. My mother had seen Mr. Trudeau, the man the whole country was talking about? Canada's sexy young prime minister?

"Did you shake his hand?"

"No, I couldn't get close enough. Oh, Mariam, I'll never forget it for the rest of my life," she gasped. "A helicopter circled above the crowd. Somebody threw buttons out of the helicopter and we all ran to get them. I was lucky I caught one." Mummy cleared her throat and continued.

"Then the helicopter landed in the centre of Place Ville Marie. When the door opened, Trudeau came bounding out," Mummy gushed as she told her story. "The crowd was huge. A band played but you could hardly hear them. And there were even go-go girls wearing white boots and matching red dresses. Each dress had a huge letter on the front and the girls stood in a line spelling out "T-R-U-D-E-A-U"! Can you believe it? I'm so glad I went." She took a deep breath.

"Did Papa go with you?" I asked.

"Oh no, I went with Annette, from the smocking group," she said. "It was mainly women anyway. He would've been out of place. Trudeau gave a speech, but I couldn't hear a word for all the screaming."

Mummy was like a different person. She was giddy and absolutely thrilled by her brush with Trudeaumania on that spring day.

She always loved Trudeau and was loyal to him long after the mania faded. "Trudeau had so much style, it was almost as if he wasn't Canadian."

My mother's trek to the Trudeau rally remained one of her favourite memories of the year we spent in Montréal for my father's sabbatical. She was more vibrant and seemed much happier there. The city stimulated and challenged her in a way that Victoria could not.

مریم

"I signed up for a course," said Mummy. "It's at Camosun College."

"What course did you sign up for?" asked my father, his head buried in the newspaper.

All of a sudden, he put the newspaper down and looked at my mother.

"But what about dinner? Who will let the girls in from school?"

"It's a music appreciation course. It's once a week in the afternoon but don't worry, I'll be home in time to let the girls in from school." She adopted a reassuring tone. "I think it's time I did something for myself. You're at the university all day with interesting people. All the new Americans and Europeans they've hired have brought a cosmopolitan air to the place. Our year in Montréal made me realize how stultifying Victoria is for me."

At college, Mummy learned all about different styles of music. I was particularly happy that she was suddenly aware of artists I knew and liked including Bob Dylan, the Rolling Stones, and the Mamas and the Papas. She became life-long friends with several people in the course.

She also joined the local Status of Women Action Group, or SWAG. At these meetings she was introduced to writings by Betty Friedan, Gloria Steinem, and Germaine Greer, among others. She tried to get me to read her copies of Ms. magazine, but I much preferred Glamour.

مريم

"*Izzmia*," she said to my father one morning over tea, "I've decided to learn how to drive. I'm going to use some of my inheritance money to buy myself a little car."

"You? Driving?" Papa did not sound impressed. "Last time you drove you banged my fender. You'll have to get your own car. I'm not letting you near mine."

"Weren't you listening, I said I was going to buy my own car with my money."

"Why the sudden urge to drive, Catherine? You always said driving didn't interest you."

"Things are changing. Most of the grocery stores don't deliver anymore, and the milkman is retiring. It seems like everybody has a car now so I might as well join the modern world."

"But where will we put a second car?"

Mummy gave my father an exasperated look, and said, "Get your head out of the clouds. We have a two-car garage, remember?"

And so my mother got her driver's license. She had a gentle teacher from the local driving school, who was much more patient than my father.

Mummy bought a 1970, dark green Toyota Corolla and named it Mitzi. Mitzi had roll-down manual windows, no radio, and a choke that had to be opened in order to get the engine going in the morning. Mummy and Mitzi bombed all over town. Actually, they drove very slowly; my mother was a timid driver. Going on the highway was a major expedition for her. Once I turned sixteen and got my driver's license, I drove Mitzi as well. My father's Dodge remained off-limits to everybody except him. We all knew it was his car.

مهم

On my way into the house, I scooped the mail out of the mailbox. There was a letter for my mother from the University of Victoria. I handed it to her and sat down at the kitchen table. I started to read my new issue of *Glamour* magazine.

"Oh my God!" cried my mother, putting one hand on her chest while the other one held her opened letter.

"What?" My magazine dropped to the floor. I leaned over and picked it up. "What's going on, Mummy? What does the letter say?"

"I've been admitted to the University of Victoria," my mother spoke slowly. "I can't believe it. Catherine Telik from Chapleau, Ontario, who didn't finish high school, has been admitted to university."

My mother had recently applied for a transfer from the community college where she had been taking courses for several years.

"Congratulations, Mummy, that's fantastic news." I barely looked up from my magazine. What was the big deal anyway?

And then it hit me. My father was a professor at the University and now my mother was going to be a student there. Both my parents were going to be on campus? Give me a break! The University of Victoria campus was compact, and I feared running into one or both my parents in the lobby of the library or at the pub. What if they saw me and said hello? Or worse still, joined me and my friends for a drink or a coffee? All I wanted to do was to be far away from my parents. Couldn't she wait until I graduated?

I looked at my mother. She was crying. I felt embarrassed so I handed her a tissue. I was just too young to understand the enormity of the emotions she felt.

The following fall, Catherine registered for one class. She never took more than a course per term so her progress towards her degree was extremely slow. Mummy was a good student. Long after her death, I found some of her essays she'd written for various courses. She got As on everything.

The University Centre cafeteria, in the middle of campus, was always packed. Spotting a student from one of my classes, I made my way to a table where he sat.

"Hi there, Charles, mind if I join you? This place is a zoo!"

"No problem," said Charles. "I'm just waiting for a friend of mine from my Russian history class. I was sick last week and I'm borrowing some notes." He motioned to two empty chairs. "Be my guest."

Just then, I heard a familiar voice: "Hello, Charles."

I turned around. It couldn't be – yes, it was, "Mummy!"

Charles looked at me and looked at my mother. "You're both students here? That's incredible!"

My mother rummaged in her tote bag. She pulled a file out and handed it to Charles. "Here are all my notes from last week's classes."

Charles took the folder and opened it. "Wow! Beautiful! They're typed!"

I looked at my mother. "You type your notes?"

"Yes, of course I do, Mariam. Makes it so much easier at exam time. Also, by going over my notes soon after the class, I can see if I have any gaps, or if there are things I don't understand and take care of them while the material is still fresh in my memory."

Mummy motioned to Charles and said, "You can keep them, I used carbon to make a copy when I typed them."

I was stupefied. I had read about students who retype their notes in books and articles about how to do well in university, but I never thought anybody really did it. My mother? The perfect student! That explained why she was in front of her typewriter all the time!

My mother inched towards getting her BA, making a friend or two in each course that she took and staying in touch with her professors. She always brought homemade cookies or muffins to any class get-together.

She had been afraid that she would end up in a life of domestic drudgery just like her mother. Community college and then university saved her. The spouses of many professors in my parents' social group were deeply unhappy, having given up their dreams so that their husband could get a tenured position. There were musicians, writers, teachers, and professors, all unemployed or underemployed. Never having had a career to give up, she did not suffer from dashed expectations. Learning for the sheer joy of it gave her immense satisfaction.

My mother wanted to expand and enrich her mind. The courses she took reflected her curiosity and broad interest in the world around her: Conversational Russian, The

Japanese Novel, Greek Tragedies, Modern China. Unlike me, she never took a course because it was mandatory or it fit into her schedule.

Two courses short of her degree requirement, she died in 1987.

21

That'll be One BA to Go and a Side of Montréal

Mariam, 1980

"Congratulations, Mariam! You have been admitted to the University of Victoria for the fall of 1976."

I looked at the perky counselor, confused. It had not occurred to me that I would not be admitted. *Didn't everyone sail from high school straight into university?*

I had an imaginary friend when I was five years old. My friend's name was Bunny. I don't remember much about Bunny except that he went to McGill.

With a father who was a professor, it's assumed that you and your imaginary friend will go to university. My parents had made it crystal clear that I had to get my BA before I could leave home. While I had long entertained fantasies of either becoming an architect or a lawyer, in reality, I did not know what I wanted to do. I was determined to leave Victoria and live in Montréal, New York, or someplace exciting. The most important thing was that I had to be as far away as possible from Victoria! Dalhousie University, in Halifax, was farther away than Montréal or Toronto but it was out because so many people from Halifax settled in Victoria saying it was similar. Queen's University in Kingston, one of Canada's finest, was crossed off my list because somebody said that I would love it there because it was "just like Victoria." Scratch.

My mother, like many women of her generation, did not have the opportunity to go to university. She felt that her life would have been very different. It was never clear to me exactly how a university degree would have altered her life but she hinted that she would have been more independent and somehow happier if she'd had a chance to pursue some sort of profession.

Mummy didn't necessarily see me as having a big career, but she did think that it was important for women to have a way of earning their living. "Just look at Mrs. MacDowell across the street. When her husband was diagnosed with MS and couldn't work anymore, she requalified as an intensive care nurse and went back to work to help support her family." She was impressed that our mousy neighbour had such good qualifications.

My father connected my having a BA to my eventual marriageability. He never actually came out and said it, but I don't think he ever seriously thought that I would have a career.

Since I had no idea what I wanted to do when I started university, I took an odd selection of courses – geography, math, economics, French, art. I took economics because my parents thought it would be useful for me to have an introduction to the subject that had supported our family. The professor, whose name was Andrew Magix, was no wizard in the classroom. His idea of a lecture was to read out loud from the very dull and dry textbook that we used. I was suitably uninspired and got a D. Happily for future students, Prof. Magix ended up in the provincial civil service where his ability to do harm was limited.

I had mentioned to the university counselor who came to my high school that I was interested in architecture, but the art history courses she suggested were full, so she pointed me to Art 100, Introduction to Art. I was a total misfit in this class, my artistic talent being close to zero. It was an interesting experience to do life drawing twice a week. However, I partially redeemed myself by mounting a well-regarded and original installation sculpture created out of dry-cleaning bags in the stairwell of the building where the art studio was located. This was one of the few enjoyable memories of my first year in university.

I failed calculus in the fall but took it again in the winter. The new professor was a dynamic young PhD from Montréal and I had a great tutor, so I made it through with a B+. I'm not sure why I took French, but I think it was part of some vague dream I had of eventually moving to Montréal. The only course I found remotely interesting was geography where I met a redheaded guy named Barry who would become my boyfriend for the next year or so.

It was an unhappy and cranky time for me. Years later, my mother reminded me that I disliked having to go to classes in different buildings. The day of my final calculus exam I refused to get out of bed because I knew I would fail. My parents persuaded a nearly hysterical me that I had to go and that if I failed it was not going to be the end of the world.

The University of Victoria was a fairly small place in 1980. A few months before I started university my father became Dean of the Faculty of Arts and Science, the faculty that I was studying in. This made my life as a student even more difficult because I felt all the pressure of being the "dean's daughter." Hardly any of my professors said anything but there would always be a pause after my name was called. I always knew why.

I hated university and felt trapped. I did not know what I wanted to do and taking a year off or transferring to another university out of town were not options. I knew I could not leave Victoria until I had completed the essential BA. In May 1977, right after I finished my first year of University, I went to Pakistan with my father. We had some long talks, and it was on his suggestion that I took up sociology. Papa thought it might be a good fit. I wasn't crazy about sociology, but it was better than anything I had taken in my first year. Another advantage was that to get a major in sociology the course requirements were low enough to allow me to take classes in political science and Asian studies as electives.

My second year went a lot better. Sociology was okay. I really liked political science and made some neat new friends. I looked into transferring to UBC in Vancouver but faced massive opposition from my parents. I was itching to be independent, but it was clear to me that I had to wait until I had my BA to leave.

Friends with apartments left me the keys when they went home for Christmas. I used to love just being alone in their empty places. Sometimes, I even bought groceries and entertained my friends. I loved it.

مریم

I had an old trunk in my room, which I filled with stuff for my future apartment. One day I came home from my summer job with a big shopping bag. Papa didn't notice things very much but on this day he did, and he wanted to know what I had bought. The bag was full of dishes. He hit the roof. From then on, I hid all my purchases from my father.

I saved my money and slowly prepared to leave home. The last year of my four-year BA in Victoria was excruciating. I limped home from classes every day, slumped in a chair in the living room, and blasted Bowie's *Ziggy Stardust* or Joni Mitchell's *Court and Spark* on the headphones. These two albums kept me going. Dying to leave my parents' house, I was allowed out one night a week with a 1 a.m. curfew. My other outings were monitored closely. If my father happened to see me at the library hanging with friends, I would be accused of socializing rather than studying and access to the car was denied to me. I longed for my independence, to live alone and keep my own hours.

After completing my third year of university, I decided to pursue a career in international development. I also reasoned that I should give economics another try because it was relevant to international development studies. There was another introductory class, taught by one of the senior administrators at the University that was supposed to be good, so I took it in my fourth year. The instructor's enthusiasm was infectious, and not only did I enjoy economics, but I did very well. I decided to do a second BA in economics and applied to both U of T and McGill.

I was more sophisticated; my personal style and my self-confidence both evolved. It's the difference between being seventeen and twenty. At the beginning of my third year at the University of Victoria, I met Julia, a tall intelligent blonde woman from Calgary. We struck up a fast friendship and I became part of her circle. Julia was hip. The summer after my third year of university she got a job at Victoria's chicest nightclub where she met Victoria's jet set – and so did I.

In a matter of weeks, Julia became the most popular girl in town and I tagged along. Through her I met people in Victoria like Nigel and Duncan, brothers who worked at British Importers and George Straith, two of Victoria's stuffiest and snobbiest clothing stores. They owned their own home. They made pasta. Duncan had a shawl-collared tuxedo from Saville Row in London and fatuously boasted about his love of Shakespeare. They acted and talked like they were from the British aristocracy, but they were just

Victoria boys who sold clothes, dressed well, and put on vapid airs. But they were amusing.

All of a sudden Victoria didn't seem too bad. I was having fun for the first time in my life and people appreciated my sophistication and ambition. I met people who had travelled. There was a girl who had lived in Paris, another one who worked for CP Air and who was fluently bilingual, and a fashion model in London who came back to Victoria to visit her mother. I had never imagined that Victoria was home to such people. The social life was amazing – private tennis tournaments, chichi dinners, hanging out at Victoria's best bars and restaurants, and fantastic parties – the most memorable of which was a "Come as your favourite fantasy" themed soirée. I went as Scarlett O'Hara and spoke in a southern drawl all night.

My father detested Julia and did everything he could to discourage my friendship with her. He called her a "man-eater" and felt she was a bad influence on me. Papa feared that I loved being with the Victoria jet set so much that I would choose to be a social butterfly rather than pursue my studies in Montréal or Toronto.

Papa needn't have fretted about my plans going astray because I was extremely determined to get out of Victoria – jet set or no jet set. My plan was to go to U of T for two years, get my economics BA and then get a job with the civil service in Ottawa. From my summer student experience with the BC government, I knew government jobs were good for women.

U of T refused to accept most of my transfer credits from Victoria. This meant that a second BA would take three years rather than two. So I decided to go to McGill, which was more generous. All this happened mere weeks after the 1980 referendum on Québec sovereignty. People in Victoria thought I was absolutely crazy to go to Montréal. I met a girl at UVIC who had left Montréal months before. She said that there was "nobody left" in Montréal. What was I getting myself into?

Papa refused to talk about me leaving home. He was mad when I got my letter of acceptance from McGill. He was unapproachable and hostile whenever I broached the topic.

I graduated from the University of Victoria in May 1980 with a BA in sociology. My father signed my diploma because he was the dean at the time. Ironically, this ensured that he was at my graduation ceremony. Had he not been dean, he never would have been there.

My father and I were scheduled to go to Pakistan on a family trip in early August and would return a week before Labour Day. As the summer of 1980 passed, I began to prepare for McGill. I paid for my first term fees and I chose one of the cheaper basement rooms at the Royal Victoria College, McGill's only all-female residence, and sent the cheque for $2600 in late July 1980. I had been saving money from my good summer jobs for years, anticipating problems with my father. For the past three years I had worked on Saturdays at the University of Victoria Library and relied on this experience to apply for jobs at the McGill libraries. Before the end of August, I had already lined up a part-time position at McGill's Redpath Library. I figured that with my room and board already paid for the entire academic year, this job would be enough to provide me with the money I needed for books and spending.

My father had a completely irrational attitude regarding my departure for McGill. At the last minute he decided to become supportive.

Labour Day weekend, I took the early morning flight to Vancouver and then on to Toronto and Montréal. I called my parents from each stop; I had travelled widely but never by myself. I had brought two large red suitcases and a beauty case filled with all my toiletries and make up. In those days before suitcases with wheels it was all very awkward and I was glad when I finally arrived, late on Saturday night, at the front desk of the Royal Victoria College at the corner of University and Sherbrooke Street. I unpacked some of my luggage and lay in bed listening to the sounds of a Montréal Saturday night in the late summer. It was thrilling.

The next day I started to meet some of my fellow residents. It was very international. I met several girls from India whose parents worked at the World Bank in Washington. I ate my first dinner in Montréal, at a Polish restaurant. I started to walk everywhere, which was something new for me since in Victoria I biked or took the car. Soon my feet were covered in blisters.

The Tuesday after Labour Day weekend was Registration Day. I had to go to the Department of Economics and make sure I was admitted into the honours programme. I was so excited that I didn't take the shortcut through campus, which would have been easier on my wounded feet. Instead, I walked out of RVC, went down University Street and then along Sherbrooke Street until I reached the main gates of

McGill, known as the Roddick Gates. This was where my parents had run into each other two decades earlier. I stood there for a minute and looked at the beautiful campus. Then I smiled and walked up the main driveway to the Leacock Building.

As I waited in the corridor to see the honours advisor, I observed the other students. They were all so urbane! They carried chic leather briefcases and wore tight jeans, and the women were in heels. I felt small town with my tote bag and low-heeled sandals.

After I registered in the honours programme, I wrote my mother a quick note and asked her to mail me an old leather briefcase of my father's. On the way home I stopped by a store that was closing down where I got myself some hot pink corduroy pants. Things were improving.

I made my basement room into a little apartment. I had my own telephone! I bought a kettle to make tea and hot chocolate as well as cookies. Soon after I arrived, my father sent me some money for a new winter coat, boots, and a cassette player. Mummy dispatched a pair of old curtains from home and a bedspread.

The reason that I had got a room at the Royal Victoria College for Women, known as RVC, was to put my father at ease, knowing I was in a place where no boys were allowed. But it was 1980 and boys were welcome to spend the night at RVC if they could fit into the tiny bed that each girl was allocated. Some girls even brought their beau to breakfast, to the delight of all the residents who got to check him out! I was one of the savvy girls who made sure all serious boyfriends had their own apartment.

By the end of the year, I was totally in love with McGill and with Montréal. I didn't want to go back to Victoria ever again. I was enthralled by the way people accepted my background – so different from Victoria. I met friends who challenged me and who opened up my world.

RVC was fun and it was a good introduction to Montréal and to McGill but by the end of the first year there, I wanted out. I hated the food and really wanted to run my own life. I was nearly twenty-two years old. Papa was opposed to me having an apartment – his big concern was boys. He wanted me to return to RVC, but I refused. My parents' old friend, my Aunt Beth, who lived in Montréal and with whom I had been in touch all year, stood up for me on this issue. She talked to my father on the telephone and told him how mature she found me. I had worked hard, maintained my honours status, and worked part-time too.

"I think it's time that you trust your daughter," she said, and Papa relented. I found my first apartment a few days later – it was just around the corner and was a studio in a high-rise building full of McGill students. I signed a lease for August 1, 1981. The rent was $160 a month including heating and electricity.

I went home to Victoria in early May 1981. The BC Ministry of Education had rehired me for the summer. Evenings and weekends I prepared for my apartment, sewing a quilt, curtains, and scouring second-hand stores for kitchen items. My plan was to box up everything I had collected and send it, air freight, to my new apartment in Montréal. All I would need to buy was a bed, a table, and a couple of chairs. I didn't need a desk or a bookshelf because I never studied at home. I worked in the library.

One Saturday in August, I drove out to Victoria airport in Mummy's Toyota stuffed with seven large boxes. I had written to the janitor of the building telling him they were on their way and asking him to put them in my apartment.

Several weeks later, I took a taxi from where the airport bus left me near the Mount Royal Hotel. I felt my heart beating as I asked the taxi driver to take me to my new apartment building on Lorne Avenue near McGill. I stopped by the janitor's apartment to get my key and holding it tightly in my hand, took the elevator up to the seventh floor. I put the key in the lock for number 701 and turned it. I slowly walked into my own apartment. My boxes were neatly piled inside.

I unpacked my small cassette player, put in a tape, and pressed "play." I opened the sliding glass door that was the only source of light and air in that small apartment. "Bette Davis eyes … !" came pulsating out of those small speakers. I started dancing around my apartment. I was ecstatic, delirious. This was my own apartment. I was finally in charge of my own life!

22

That Black Man

Catherine and Izzud-Din Pal, my parents,
on their wedding day, May 3, 1957.

No way in hell I was going to Irish Uncle's memorial service by myself. I wanted to support his widow Big B, my maternal aunt, but I was apprehensive. Most of the family, my late mother's siblings, would be there. Facing them alone was a sobering prospect. I wasn't yet married, so there was no husband to accompany me. No boyfriend, either. A bodyguard seemed a bit over the top. There was a fourth option: a handsome gay man. Dennis was drop-dead gorgeous, smart, and had an extensive wardrobe of suits for his corporate job in downtown Montréal. Most importantly, he was charming and witty. Dennis could handle the family.

"Of course, Mariam, I'd be delighted to be your beard," said Dennis.

I checked the box "accompanied" on my invitation card, sealed the envelope, and off it went to Kingston.

The service took place on the first day of summer – a glorious June morning with a perfect blue sky. Dennis picked me up, coffees in hand, and soon we were zooming down the highway to Ontario.

We coordinated our outfits. The family was a pretty dowdy bunch, and I didn't want to fit in. Dennis wore a navy suit, crisp white shirt, elegant Italian silk tie, loafers, and a straw hat with a navy stripe. I was in pearls, a white linen top, and a blue-and-white linen skirt. I carried a pink designer bag and wore navy pumps. For a bit of dramatic flair, I added a black straw *chapeau* with an enormous tulle bow in the back. If fashion can be used as a shield, then I felt fully protected.

I took my hat off, carefully placed it on the rear seat, and leaned back. As Québec curved into Ontario, I told Dennis what to expect.

"Now, let me fill you in on some family history. My mother was the eldest of seven . . ."

Mummy had two brothers and four sisters. She left her home in the small Northern Ontario town of Chapleau for Toronto in 1947 where she joined a theatre troupe. Dreaming of becoming an actress, she was determined to go to London, England. My grandfather funded her 1950 transatlantic passage and sent her money while she was there. Two years later, having not set foot on the stage, she returned to Chapleau. I'm not sure what happened. I do know that her father had run out of funds and could no longer subsidize her.

A man of modest means who worked as a CPR carpenter, my grandfather spent a considerable amount of his savings on my mother. This unfortunate lack of planning meant that he was unable to help the remaining six children with their higher education. To make things worse, he died in 1954, leaving his widow with only a modest pension. Regrettably, Mummy's siblings resented her.

Mummy paid for her father's poor judgment for the rest of her life. To atone for his sins, she helped two of her sisters with their educations. When she met my father, she shared an apartment with a sister and brother to keep costs down. It was never enough.

"They complained bitterly when I married because their rent increased," recalled Mummy.

مریم

Summer road construction delays meant we were amongst the last to arrive for the memorial. We parked far away. I put my hat back on and grabbed my bag. Dennis and I strolled up the long driveway to Big B's house.

Irish Uncle's son and daughter from his previous marriage were seated at a table just outside the front door. I introduced Dennis and we signed the guest book.

I noticed two people around my age standing nearby. They looked at us, eyes squinting in the bright summer sun. "Long lost cousins?" I wondered aloud as Dennis ambled over with his hand out and introduced himself.

"Nice to meet you, Peter. Nice to meet you, Max," Dennis said as they shook hands. Oh, he's Mabel's son. From Oregon.

I smiled and held out my hand to Peter. "I'm Catherine's daughter, Mariam. Mariam Pal from Montréal." Peter's hand stayed in his pocket.

He looked at me for a second. "Yes. I know who you are." Then he started to walk away from the house.

I slowly lowered my right hand and turned to Dennis. Without missing a beat, he took me by the left and guided me inside the house. He shrugged, laughed, and whispered, "Things are starting off well, my dear!"

Mabel was the second oldest. Mummy and Mabel had a toxic relationship for most of their lives. The two sisters stopped talking to each other in 1955. I asked Mummy several times why their relationship was so bad, but I never got a clear answer.

"Mabel was always very jealous of me," said Mummy. "She thought I was prettier than her. When she heard that I married your father, she couldn't stand it. Within a couple of years, she also married a professor. He got a job in Oregon and she spent most of her life there." Mummy shrugged.

"I used to get news of Mabel through my sister Elizabeth. Then out of the blue, in the late '70s, Mabel wrote me. I replied, and we corresponded. We met twice after that – and both times were tense."

Even though Mabel lived in Montréal when my parents married, she was the only sibling who never met my father. I am not sure why.

According to my parents and an old family friend, Mabel convinced my maternal grandmother, Wilhelmina, not to call my mother (and me) when she visited Montréal shortly after my birth. Mummy confided in a letter that Wilhelmina referred to my father as "that black man my daughter married." She returned to Chapleau, Ontario without ever seeing her daughter and granddaughter.

The family did not approve of their lovely, hazel-eyed, pale Kate marrying the brown man from Pakistan. Accepting me implied accepting my father and my mother's marriage. They never did. My mere existence brought out their deep displeasure and discomfort with Mummy's choice of spouse. Most of the family doesn't know anything about me, nor do they care.

I met Mabel twice. The first time was a year after Mummy died when Mabel, my Aunt Elizabeth, and Big B came to Montréal to visit my mother's grave. I was thirty. Afterwards, we went for tea. Mabel was dismayed that she had never known me as I was growing up. She made it sound like it was my mother's doing. This got under my skin.

I had to say something.

"You know, it's not my fault that there was no contact. I was just a child. Why didn't you patch things up? Why didn't you try to get along for the sake of your children?"

Mabel looked at me, silent. My other two aunts stared at the floor. I knew I had crossed a line but after a lifetime of rejection by the family I needed to speak up.

Twenty years would go by before I saw her again.

Mabel had spotted me. I watched her swagger through the living room. She came to a full stop about two feet away, folded her arms, and looked up at me like a cat about to drink a saucer of cream.

"So do you consider yourself to be a Muslim?" Mabel asked after a perfunctory hello. We both knew the answer.

"Yes, I do." I smiled.

"How can you be a Muslim, a feminist, and identify with what all those Islamic terrorists do in the name of religion?"

Mabel was no diplomat. I wasn't going to give her the satisfaction of having a conversation about this. Dennis winked at me from the buffet. He sauntered over, in rescue mode.

"Well, the situation is more complicated than most Americans realize. Just like Christians, there are many kinds of Muslims. I would say the majority of Muslims condemn this perverted and medieval form of the religion."

Mabel uncrossed her arms. She was just about to speak when Dennis arrived. He flashed her a winning smile.

"Oh, hi, Dennis. I'd like you to meet my late mother's sister, Mabel." There was no way I would refer to that woman as my aunt.

Mabel shook Dennis's hand and gave him an appraising look.

"The two of you certainly make a nice couple."

"Thank you very much. Dennis, shall we circulate some more?"

I turned my head towards Mabel. "Nice talking to you!"

We left her standing there not quite knowing what had just happened.

I was nibbling on a small egg salad sandwich when a woman came running up to me. She had a huge smile on her face.

"Hello, Mariam? I am your Aunt Annette. I recognized you immediately! You have your mother's smile." Moments later her husband, my Uncle William, appeared by her side and we talked for a while. I hadn't seen him since I was eleven years old when our family visited Chapleau. An engineer with CP Rail, William was the only one who stayed in his hometown.

Mummy's other brother, Thomas, was at the memorial. I first met him in the late 1980s at Big B's. His wife came up to me and said in a loud voice that reminded me of Ethel Merman, "Hello, I'm your Aunt Caroline."

Retired from the Air Force, Uncle Thomas and Caroline lived in Ottawa. I see them from time to time but sense their distance.

Two sisters did not attend – Elizabeth and Heather. Elizabeth and Mummy had maintained contact. She lived in Ottawa with her husband John. Elizabeth's health was very bad for many years: vision problems and depression kept her hospitalized for long stretches of time. Her sister-in-law raised one of her two children, as Elizabeth was too sick to look after them.

Elizabeth's daughter, Janet, came to visit Victoria when Papa and I were on one of our trips to Pakistan. When Mummy asked her not to chain-smoke inside the house, Janet got mad. The next day, a taxi pulled up outside the house to take her to the airport. That was how my stunned mother found out that Janet was leaving a week early.

Heather was the baby of the family; too young to know her eldest sister. Mabel brought her to Oregon. Heather got her teeth fixed, trained as a hairdresser, had a huge falling out with Mabel, and married an American guy named Joe. Driving a massive motorhome, she and her husband and dog, Oliver, showed up in Victoria when I was in my mid-teens. Heather wore high heels and halter dresses, plenty of makeup, had long scarlet nails, and constantly chewed gum.

"She looked like a cow, chewing all day long," said Mummy. I could hardly believe that she and Mummy were sisters.

I knew that Mummy and Big B had been very close. Of all her siblings, Mummy seemed to miss her the most. In the '70s they got back in touch. I was curious to meet her. One day in 1983 or 1984 when I was in Toronto, I looked up her number and called. She was floored when I told her who was on the phone. We've been close friends ever since.

Yet the tension bubbles just beneath the surface. When my comatose mother was hospitalized in 1987 due to a stroke that would prove fatal, I was the conduit between the family and the Pals. I faithfully called Big B with updates to share. Not one of her siblings contacted my father, my sister, or myself directly or sent flowers or a card. The family was unforgiving.

Big B then did something that would have lasting repercussions. She called the hospital and asked that her name be added to my mother's file so that she would be notified in case something happened. A nurse wrote in the file that Big B wanted to be informed directly when Mummy died, as she was not sure that we would tell her.

After Mummy's death, Papa saw this in the file and was absolutely furious. He had been warming up to Big B. Now he was through with her and her siblings. I understood my father's fury and pain. I did not approve of what she did, but I was not willing to give up my only relative on my mother's side. From that day forward I kept my relationship with her private. Papa had no idea that I attended Irish Uncle's memorial service.

مریم

When they find out about my Polish-Canadian half, some people wonder if I speak any Polish or if I have any ties to my mother's homeland. The answer is no. My father's culture loomed much larger than my mother's. I think that to a large extent this was due to Mummy's fascination and interest in Pakistan.

Mummy had tremendous affection for her heritage, which expressed itself in various ways. When she returned to university, she studied Slavic language, literature, and culture. Mummy introduced my father to dill pickles, rye bread, perogies, and pickled beets. She made borscht and the occasional cabbage roll. She questioned the strict Catholicism in which she was raised back in the late 1940s and her departure from the church had nothing to do with her marriage.

The family doesn't have particularly strong ties to Poland. They're all pretty North American. My hunch is that had they been present in my life, my cultural identity would not have been any different. Yet I'm sorry I missed out on having aunts, uncles, and cousins, and saddened that they never knew me as a child. The lingering jealousies at the heart of the rift between Mummy and the family simmered for far too long. I also wonder why none of the six siblings took their mother to task for referring to their sister's husband as a black man.

Mummy rarely talked about the agony her family caused her. For most of my life Papa never said anything good about them. Years after my mother died, I was surprised to learn from her letters how much my father had tried to get along with her siblings, inviting them for dinner and family occasions like birthdays.

The family is not bad or evil but the pain they caused my parents was both unnecessary and wrong. I'm not sure they knew any better.

Both my parents had sibling problems. Papa also had very difficult relationships with both of his brothers. I was cut off from my paternal grandfather and some of my cousins because of their feuding. Since my father died, we have all found each other again. I'm amazed by their acceptance and unconditional love. We all regret that the three brothers did not get along and resolve to be different. I see no such reflection and compassion amongst the children of my mother's siblings. They seem determined to repeat the sins of their fathers and mothers. From the reactions I elicited at the memorial, this seemed to be happening.

مريم

The memorial service was over. From start to finish it had been a fitting tribute to Irish Uncle.

Dennis and I had a magnificent time. I was proud of my performance. I did it for my parents. As we walked to the car, the blue skies clouded over, announcing a sudden change in the weather. Just as Dennis opened the car door for me, a big fat raindrop fell onto my head. Then the skies opened up. I twirled in the rain, feeling the cool drops on my skin.

"I love a summer shower. It's so cleansing," said Dennis. He turned the key in the ignition. "Let's go home."

Glossary

Acha. Okay. Yes.

Achar. Chutney made of mangoes, lemons, and limes with chilies and oil.

Aik. One(number). Aik minute – one minute.

Ammi jee. Grandmother.

Bohut. Very, as in very good, very hot.

Chalo. Let's go!

Chapatti. A flat wheat bread common in the Punjab.

Charpai. A wood-framed rope bed, common in South Asia.

Chooridar pants. A traditional garment, pants that fit tightly below the knee and balloon from waist to knee.

Dada Abajee. Grandfather.

Daal. Lentils or pulses.

Desi. Home style. Pakistani style.

Diwali. Hindu festival of lights.

Dupatta. A diaphanous scarf, made of a light transparent fabric, worn on the head and shoulders, to complete the female *shalwar kameeze.*

Eid. There are two *Eid* celebrations. One is for *Eid-ul-Fitr,* at the end of *Ramadan,* a month of fasting. The other is *Eid-al-Adha,* which commemorates the story of Ibrahim and Isak.

Firunghi. Literally, foreigner.

Ghazals. Love poems set to music.

Halal. Meat killed in accordance with Islamic tradition. Similar to Kosher.

Haveli. The traditional Muslim house of North India and Pakistan.

Heera mandi. The red-light district.

Hookah. Water pipe.

Jaldi. Hurry up!

Khosas. Traditional handmade leather shoes worn in Punjab.

Lakh. Traditional Punjabi measure meaning 100,000.

Lunghi. Ankle length loincloth worn by men in Punjab.

Madrassa. A school located in a mosque.

Naan. A flat wheat bread cooked in a traditional tandoor oven.

Namkeen chai. Kashmiri tea made with green tea, milk, and salt

Paan. A mildly narcotic confection made of betel nut.

Punkah. A handheld or ceiling fan operated by pulling a cord.

Purdah. Literally means "Veil" and refers to the seclusion of women from unrelated men.

Raita. Yogurt mixed with mint, cucumber, tomato, and cumin seed.

Ramadan. A month in the Islamic calendar when Muslims are to refrain from eating and drinking from dawn until dusk.

Sahib. Sir.

Shalwar kameez. Outfit worn by women and men in South Asia. It consists of baggy pants and a tunic.

Sharm. Shame, a South Asian concept tied to one's conformity to social standards and norms.

Tonga. A two-wheeled horse drawn cart.

Acknowledgements

I was fortunate to have several wonderful writing instructors who helped me find my voice and taught me how to express it better: Wendell Capili, Mark Abley, and Maria Turner.

I would like to thank Marjorie Simmons for her comprehensive and useful edit of an earlier draft. Her excellent suggestions helped me to prepare a more polished final manuscript. Licia Canton provided extremely helpful comments on several chapters of an even earlier version. Guy Naysmith and Laurie Johnson read and commented on drafts of several chapters set in Victoria. My close friends patiently listened while I read my work to them out loud, often in noisy restaurants.

A huge hug and thank you to my dear husband Eli who patiently read and reread all of the chapters. And this book never would have been completed without the pithy comments of the members of my writing group who have included, since 2013, Karen Zey, Prue Rains, Rita Pomade, Claire Hellman, Chris Galvin, and Manoosh Valipour.

My thanks as well to Lawrence Clemen for his kind assistance scanning all the photos included in the book.

I am also grateful to Renaissance Press for their support and for believing in a first-time author.

Mariam S. Pal
November 2021

About the Author

Born in Montréal, Mariam Pal spent her childhood in Victoria, BC, where *Ballet is not for Muslim Girls* is set. Mariam returned to Montréal to live four decades ago. She has degrees in economics and law from McGill. A former resident of Abidjan, Cote d'Ivoire, and Manila, Philippines, Mariam has traveled extensively in Europe, Asia, and Africa. She is retired from careers in economic development and immigration law and lives in Montréal with her musician husband, Eli. In retirement she grows garlic, bakes a mean focaccia bread, and is working on her second book *Eating Pineapple Upside Down Cake in Monrovia*.

If you enjoyed this book,
you might enjoy these other Renaissance titles

AFRICANTHOLOGY

Perspectives of Black Canadian Poets
Edited by A. Gregory Frankson

Truth spoken plainly and powerfully is difficult to dismiss and impossible to ignore. Edited by Greg Frankson, *AfriCANthology: Perspectives of Black Canadian Poets* brings together some of Canadas most influential dub, page, and spoken word poetic voices and gives them space to speak freely about their personal journeys in piercing verse and unapologetic prose. Just as individual experiences of Blackness are diverse across Canada, each contributor recounts aspects of navigating their unique personal, professional, and artistic paths in Black skin with fearless candour and audacious forthrightness.

WITH CONTRIBUTIONS BY

Afua Cooper, Reed "iZrEAL" Jones, Evelyn C. White, Thandiwe McCarthy, Aly Ndiaye|Webster, Chloé Savoie-Bernard, Rodney St. Éloi, Jamaal Amir Akbari, Dwayne Morgan, Andrea Thompson, Asante Haughton, George Elliot Clarke, Olive Senior, Truth Is..., Bertrand Bickersteth, Valerie Mason-John, Cicely Belle Blain, Wayde Compton

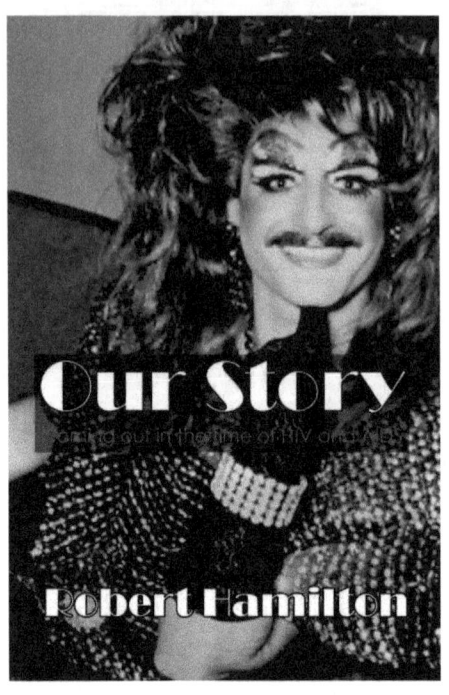

Our Story

Coming Out in the Time of HIV and AIDS
By Robert Hamilton

This is a story of friendship, love, loss, and drag told with humour and compassion. In 1977, the author, goes in search of his gay self. After beginning his career as a prison guard, he timidly comes out into the gay scene, where a lasting and sometimes tumultuous friendship develops with Joe, a drag queen. Their world changes when they're swept into the eye of the AIDS storm, a time when testing positive for HIV was considered a death sentence.

This is an intimate look at the impact AIDS had on the author's family of gay friends and those around them.

www.ingramcontent.com/pod-product-compliance
Lightning Source LLC
Chambersburg PA
CBHW070909120626
46546CB00001B/193